IN
WASHINGTON
BUT NOT
OF IT

IN WASHINGTON BUT NOT OF IT

The Prophetic Politics
of
Religious Lobbyists

DANIEL J. B. HOFRENNING

Temple University Press, Philadelphia

Temple University Press, Philadelphia 19122
Copyright © 1995 by Temple University
Published 1995

⊗ The paper used in this book meets the requirements of the
American National Standard for Information Sciences—Permanence of
Paper for Printed Library Materials, ANSI Z39.48-1984

Printed in the United States of America

Text design by Charles Field

Library of Congress Cataloging-in-Publication Data

Hofrenning, Daniel J. B.
    In Washington but not of it : the prophetic politics of religious
lobbyists / Daniel J.B. Hofrenning.
        p.   cm.
    Includes bibliographical references (p.   ) and index.
    ISBN 1-56639-303-5 (cloth). — ISBN 1-56639-304-3 (pbk.)
    1. Religion and politics—United States–History–20th century.
2. Lobbying—United States.   3. United States—Religion—20th
century.   4. United States—Politics and government—20th century.
I. Title.
BL2525.H65   1995
324′.4′0882—dc20   94-49061

For Nancy and Theo

CONTENTS

ACKNOWLEDGMENTS

In completing this project, I have been assisted in innumerable ways by many people. Among my academic colleagues, Virginia Gray read many drafts and made my work immeasurably clearer. Barbara Nelson provided inspiration when the journey seemed long and also made helpful criticisms of the entire text. Frank Sorauf worked to sharpen the overall argument and continually reminded me that social scientists must be good writers. Martin Marty insightfully reviewed the entire manuscript. In addition to these people, Jo Beld, Nancy Brown, Erling Jorstad, James Hofrenning, Ted Jelen, L. DeAne Lagerquist, Phil Shively, Gary Stansell, Matthew Moen, and Paul Weber read and provided comments on all or part of the text. Finally, my students in Political Science 115, "Religion and Politics," read the text and provided many fresh and beneficial comments. Following that class, Grete Larson, Sue Ward, Bob Deward, Chris Kaufman, Ginny Kingman, Matt Braaten, and Christa Van Gundy read and commented on all or part of the text. Though each of these people would undoubtedly seek additional changes, my work was improved by their suggestions.

Temple University Press provided invaluable support. I especially thank Doris Braendel for guiding and supporting this project from beginning to end. In addition, Carolyn

Jones and anonymous reviewers made particularly thorough and helpful comments on the entire text. Peter Reinhart and Bill Stavru provided careful and meticulous editorial work that solved many problems. Eric Banks compiled the index.

I thank the Society for the Scientific Study of Religion for providing a research grant that financed a portion of the fieldwork. In addition, John, Doris, Stephanie, and Darcy Skarsten; Roy Enquist; John Lillie; Donna Anderson; Edna Kelly; and Arnold Keller all provided or helped secure housing and office space while I was conducting interviews in Washington. In Washington, thanks also are due to the people I have called religious lobbyists. They generously and graciously gave of their time and allowed me to interview them. It was a privilege to enter their world and hear their stories.

As the work was being completed, my colleagues in the political science department at Saint Olaf College provided helpful criticism of portions of the project. Shawn Paulson, Kari Waddington, and Jaimie Schillinger provided critical clerical support. I look forward to continued collaboration.

Of course, I must thank the most important people in my life, my family. My parents, Jim and Ing, and my siblings, Peter and Kathy, provided much support. In our home, they sparked my interest in religion and politics during countless conversations around the dinner table and elsewhere. Even more importantly, they always believed in me. That support has made the difference.

I save my most profound gratitude for my wife, Nancy Brown, whom I married at the beginning of this project. I thank her for providing unending support, for tolerating my distractions, and for editing the entire manuscript. As always, she showed me the extraordinary power of words. Finally, our son, Theo, arrived to Nancy and me near the end of this endeavor and provides intense joy. To Nancy and Theo, I dedicate this book.

1
CHAPTER

Religious Lobbyists as Prophets

Organized religion has played a vital role in virtually every major political issue in the history of the United States. During the Revolution, ministers were in the throes of the struggle for independence. Most supported the Revolution and often boldly proclaimed their support of liberty from the pulpit. But, as in most struggles, organized religion was found on both sides. Some clergy, perhaps 25 percent, maintained an allegiance to the crown. After the Revolution, as they forged a new nation, virtually all the American founders thought religion was essential to the republic. Although they feared that religion could threaten liberty, the early leaders contended that religion provided an indispensable source of morality for the new nation's citizens. Democracy might not survive without it.

Religion has continued to play a significant part in many other issues of public significance. The movement to end slavery began in a Quaker meeting house. The Progressive and Populist movements drew much energy and support from organized religion. The prohibition of alcohol was in large part a religious movement. The protest against the Vietnam War included many prominent religious leaders at its forefront. In recent years, battles over abortion and Nicaraguan Contra aid would have changed considerably without the involvement of religious groups. In virtually every significant issue of American public life, religion has been inextricably involved.

Despite this involvement, many analyses of American politics ignore the role of religion. The major media seem blind to the significance of religion. When Martin Luther King, Jr., was assassinated, a television announcer reported, "And so today there was a memorial service for the slain civil rights leader, Dr. Martin Luther King, Jr. It was a religious service, and it is fitting that it should be, for, after all, Dr. King was the son of a minister."[1] Reporting of this type depreciates the religious identity of the civil rights movement. Martin Luther King, Jr., was indeed the son of a minister, but he himself was also a minister. Every speech he made was shaped by his own personal faith, his academic study of theology, and the oral tradition of black preaching. In the civil rights movement that he led, virtually all the organizational meetings, all the rallies, all the celebrations, all the funerals were held in churches. Religion gave the civil rights movement the impulse to take on injustice and the sustenance to endure through the long struggle. To ignore this dimension is nothing less than a failure to understand the heart of one of the most important political movements of the twentieth century.[2]

In academia scholars have often minimized religion by placing it in the framework of secularization theory. In this theory, religion shrinks in value as societies advance toward modernity.[3] Advancing human reason increasingly makes religion unneccesary. "This theory or myth is that of the Enlightenment, which views science as the bringer of light relative to which religion and other dark things will vanish away."[4] From this perspective, religion is a primitive practice. Some evidence supports the secularization theory. In most countries of Western Europe, surely among the most "modern," organized religion seems to have faded. Fewer and fewer Europeans attend worship services or engage in other religious practices. In the United States, some public opinion polls show higher rates of religious observance among people who live in rural areas and have lower levels of education. One might argue that these people have less exposure to modernizing forces in society.[5]

However, much evidence belies the secularization theory. In the United States and elsewhere, religion persists and flourishes amid modernization. Viewing the world through the lens of secularization theory, scholars ignore or explain away evidence of the powerful allure of religion for all people.[6] As a result, they fail to comprehend why 90 percent of Americans continue to tell pollsters that they believe in God.[7] They may misunderstand international affairs by ignoring the central role of religion in two-thirds of the seventy armed conflicts in the world today.[8] They do not understand Hillary Clinton's talk of America's "sleeping sickness of the soul"[9] or the millions who flocked to the candidacies of Pat Robertson and Jesse Jackson.

The media and scholars have also failed to assess the rich variety of religious groups that has recently become involved in the political process. Though religion has always been a part of U.S. politics, evidence suggests that there has been a recent upsurge in religious involvement. In the 1960s, the activity of religious liberals in the Civil Rights Movement and the protest against the Vietnam War was the big story. In the 1980s and 1990s, conservative religious organizations thundered onto the political stage with concerns about school prayer, abortion, education, and gay rights. Some of these groups have literally served as precinct caucuses for the Republican party.[10] The religious "left" remained active on many issues including South African apartheid and conflict in Central America; however, the religious right was more vigorous. Interestingly, religious groups have become active when many citizens expressed much cynicism and apathy about American politics. Other forms of political participation such as voting and involvement with political parties declined. The two trends may be connected. While other forms of participation have deteriorated, organized religion has moved to fill the void.

Responses to the contemporary politicization of religion have been mixed. At the Republican convention of 1992, many people decried the dominant role of religious conservatives. Some of the critics were fellow Republicans who resented the entry of these zealous new religious activists. Some Republicans formed the Republican Majority Coalition, an organization aimed at revitalizing the more moderate and less explicitly religious wing of the party. Toward the other end of the political spectrum, Molly Yard, former president of the National Organization for Women, recently said, "Political leaders would do well to understand the ominous threat of the church."[11]

Other contemporary commentators take a more balanced approach. Responding to the rage over the spirited role of groups like the Moral Majority and the Christian Coalition, David Broder argues that the hysteria is overstated. No single religious group dominates the political process and imposes its will on all citizens. Pointing to groups as diverse as Affirmation, a voice for gay and lesbian Mormons, and the Friends Coordinating Committee on Peace, Broder concludes, "The endless variety is reassuring, for it reflects the diversity in our society, which many incorrectly feel is threatened whenever some man or movement of strong religious faith appears on the political scene."[12]

In the midst of this increasing activism, not all scholars have ignored religion. Many have moved to broader understanding of religion and politics. In the last few years, political scientists and sociologists have done more research on the role of religion in politics. Sociologists Robert Wuthnow and James Davidson Hunter have published pathbreaking books on religion, politics, and society that have received wide acclaim.[13] In political science, a sizable number of books and articles have been published in the last five

years.[14] Scholars are increasingly realizing the integral role
of religion in American politics.

This book examines a particularly neglected aspect of religion in U.S. politics, religious lobbying. While there have
been many studies of lobbying in general, few scholars or
other observers have focused on religious lobbying. Using
other studies of lobbying, I will compare religious lobbyists
with their secular counterparts and assess their role in the
American political process. I will argue that religious lobbyists significantly transform politics in the United States, but
that they wield power in ways distinct from other political
actors. In terms of conventional wins and losses on specific
pieces of legislation, religious lobbyists often—but not always—come up short. Occasionally they achieve momen-
tous legislative victories, but their influence transcends any
simple tally of wins and losses. They are also powerful because of their clarion calls for moral reform. With these
calls, religious lobbyists register a challenge to the state and
offer mediating organizations for citizens to voice their discontent.

In a country in which church and state are separate, the
existence of this religious challenge is not surprising. The
purposeful design of religious institutions distinct from the
state will inevitably produce challenges to the state. This
arrangement enhances democracy; indeed, the preservation
of democracy depends upon the existence of autonomous
organizations.[15] Garry Wills states, "That is one of the
American paradoxes that we can be most proud of—that
our churches have influence because they are independent
of any government."[16] Without the organization of groups
in opposition to the state, a government can become tyran-
nical, and religious lobbies are among the organizations
that arise to challenge the state. While similar in some respects to other, nonreligious organizations, their religious
roots make them unique. Because religion has long been a
primary source of moral and ethical teaching, religious lob-

byists play an important and distinctive role in the maintenance of liberty and justice in the American experiment.

THE PROPHETIC POLITICS OF RELIGIOUS LOBBYISTS

Lobbying is an important political activity of organized religion. In the last half century, a growing number of
churches, synagogues, and religious organizations have established lobbying offices in Washington. Ironically, the
very idea of religious lobbying seems incongruous to some.
The serene and contemplative rituals of religion seem a far
cry from the rough and tumble of politics. The popular media and populist politicians groan about the pernicious impact of lobbying, pointing to fantastic expense accounts and
slick salespersons for the rich and powerful. To many observers, lobbyists are people who lavish campaign contributions, expense-paid trips, and so-called lecture fees on legislators in exchange for parochial legislation that undermines
the broader public interest.

   The recent scandals of prominent television evangelists
and other religious leaders might lead us to assume that
religious lobbyists are no more principled than nonreligious
lobbyists. Nor would we be the first to reach this conclusion. Looking further back in history, religion's seamier
side is evident. Slavery and apartheid endured in part because of religious justifications. Many of the purges and in-
quisitions of centuries past had religious inspiration. While
not denying that religion has sometimes been a force for ill,
this book argues that contemporary religious lobbyists offer
a principled and moralistic vision. Unlike most other lobbyists, they seek nothing less than a transformation of American politics to a higher moral plane.

   While sharing a common goal of transforming society,
religious lobbyists differ—sometimes radically—in their

political and theological beliefs. In the struggle to form U.S. policy toward Nicaragua, liberal groups vigorously fought the efforts of President Ronald Reagan's administration to increase aid to the Nicaraguan Contras. At the same time, some conservative groups were reported to have sent chaplains to minister to those very contras who fought the ruling Sandinistas. A similar paradox existed regarding policy toward South Africa. While some groups stated that one could not have true faith in God without opposing apartheid, conservative leader Jerry Falwell traveled to South Africa and attempted to discredit Archbishop Desmond Tutu and antiapartheid forces. Despite these intense differences, religious lobbyists share a common type of political strategy. They have the same approach because of their shared religious heritage and their similar relationship to the state. All religious lobbyists claim a Jewish and Christian tradition[17] that calls followers to work for morality, justice, and peace. This tradition includes ancient biblical exhortations to create "a new heaven and a *new earth.*" No other lobbyists claim such an ancient and extensive moral foundation.

In addition to their heritage, all religious lobbyists share a similar relationship to the state. They are often viewed with suspicion simply because they are religious. Other lobbyists who work on similar issues do not face the same obstacles. Legislators and citizens object to the very presence of religious lobbyists because they violate the tidy picture of a separate church and state. If church and state are deeply divergent, then some argue that religion should not be political. As a result of this sentiment, many religious lobbyists are deemed illegitimate players in Washington politics. Their common experience of rejection contributes to a type of activism that is different from nonreligious lobbying.

The word *prophetic* best describes the strategy of religious lobbyists. Many may object to the use of the word *prophet* to describe this group of activists. There are powerful differ-

ences between Old Testament prophets and religious lobbyists, but there are similarities as well. Prophets claim to
communicate directly with God. Max Weber made famous
the notion of the prophet's charismatic authority. Weber
contrasted prophetic authority that rests in the unique cha-
risma of individuals with bureaucratic authority that is
rooted in one's position in the hierarchical institutions in
society.[18] The clear implication of Weber's distinction is that
the prophet worked outside the major institutions of society.[19]

Other scholars point to the location of prophets within
the temple and other central institutions of society. Sigmund Mowinckel wrote of the existence of cults of
prophets who had an official status in ancient Israel,[20]
where the king often appointed prophets to sit in his court.
They were called on to speak the truth, no matter how disturbing or uncomfortable. Many uttered penetrating criticisms of governments that ignored the poor and practiced
other forms of injustice.[21] Because religious lobbyists are appointed by organizations and institutions to do their work,
they can be understood as contemporary "cultic prophets."
Like ancient prophets, religious lobbyists offer scathing criticisms of the state based upon their interpretation of their
religious tradition.

To be sure, religious lobbyists may be false prophets.
That is, they may claim to root their arguments in their religious tradition, but in reality their work is secular. Some
scholars have argued that creating specialized lobbying offices and other agencies may be evidence of the increasing
secularization of churches themselves. Lobbyists may work
in ancillary organizations that are superfluous to the exercise of real religious authority that takes place in congregations and synagogues. Religious lobbying is then distinguished from activity that is truly religious or prophetic.[22]

In Israel, the difficulties of discerning false prophets may
have led the temple to end the cult of prophets. Identifying

prophets of the twentieth century is difficult, but religious lobbyists act in prophetic ways. At least they understand themselves in prophetic terms. They offer searing condemnation based upon their interpretation of biblical justice. Whether false or true prophets, their criticisms are prophetic. To those who fear religious political activism, one might draw comfort in the fact that even true prophets are rarely followed. Indeed, the Scriptures note that prophets are often unacceptable in their own country, not necessarily because they are wrong, but because their truth is too distressing.

In Washington, prophetic lobbyists engage in radical as opposed to mainstream politics. Like biblical prophets, they begin with a deep dissatisfaction with the status quo. In response to their discontent, religious lobbyists seek fundamental change on a wide range of public policies. This effort contrasts with the work of most nonreligious lobbyists, who seek small changes in a narrow range of policies. Unlike their secular counterparts, religious lobbyists aspire to reorder the very priorities of government and alter the terms of the political debate. Like the long tradition of prophets before them, religious lobbyists see something profoundly wrong with society. In response, they expound an alternative vision for U.S. public policy.

Because it is prophetic, all religious lobbying—both conservative and liberal—works against a ruling elite that holds values alien to their faiths. While virtually all religious lobbyists share an antielitist perspective, different lobbyists perceive different elites as the source of America's ills. Religious conservatives blame a secular humanist elite. At a recent meeting of the Christian Coalition in Washington, D.C., Gary Bauer, president of the Family Research Council, another conservative lobbying organization, was honored as the "Protestant Layman of the Year." In his speech, he exhorted the delegates by saying, "How superior your values are to the decadent elite of this city. . . . Before this decade is over your values will prevail."[23] In the eyes of conservative Christians, the secular humanist elite have corroded the underlying values that have made America great. Family values seem particularly vulnerable. In addition, the secular humanists fail to protect the unborn or recognize the necessity of prayer in the schools.

Liberals rage against another elite. Their elite is aligned with a wealthy corporate power structure that threatens to divert resources away from the poor and needy to the rich and powerful. In the debate on the North American Free Trade Agreement, many liberal groups spoke of the corporate supporters of NAFTA who lobbied Congress heavily. One liberal activist stated,

> I think there's a special concern of churches in this country, not only about ourselves and working brothers and sisters in our communities, but also of brothers and sisters in Mexico and Canada. Why in the world doesn't President Clinton just say this is the Bush/Quayle agreement? Why doesn't he say, "Let's make this agreement right?"[24]

To religious liberals, the alliance with the corporate elite is blasphemous politics and is diametrically opposed to the prophetic demands of faith.

Because their prophetic stance often is not supported by their members, religious lobbyists are criticized for their autocratic or oligarchical tendencies. The members of such denominations as the Episcopalians and Presbyterians may not necessarily share the prophetic or antielitist political sentiments of the religious lobbyists who represent them in Washington. For example, Episcopalian lobbyists work for a fairly liberal political agenda; however, public opinion polls show that most lay Episcopalians are Republicans who disagree with the policy positions of that agenda. To a degree, prophets are only concerned with truth; the acquiescence of members is unimportant. However, a purely autocratic approach may lead members to oppose or even dismantle the budgets of offending lobbyists. Religious lobbyists need grassroots support to have influence in Washington. As a result, the internal politics of religious lobbyists are an intriguing mix of democracy and oligarchy.[25]

Religious lobbyists' prophetic perspective also puts them at odds with much of the Washington establishment. This peculiar position serves as the context for a distinctive set of political tactics. Because they challenge elite values, their access to elite lawmakers and other power brokers is limited. In many cases, religious lobbyists do not desire insider access. Contact with elites usually means bargaining and compromise, which religious lobbyists avoid. As a result, religious lobbyists tend to adopt an "outsider" strategy that allows them to operate in Washington with minimal compromise. Instead of insider access to Washington power brokers, this strategy mobilizes people at the grass roots to send letters, call their representatives, and sometimes protest and demonstrate. Religious lobbyists remain distanced from the political elite. Sometimes they engage in elite contact, but most often they work to communicate their principles to the Washington elites and try to demonstrate the power of their organization.

Religious lobbyists are not the sole practitioners of this outsider strategy; many nonreligious lobbyists share it. Religious lobbyists for causes such as the struggle against legal abortion or the movement for sanctions against the apartheid regime of South Africa have much in common with their secular allies who work for the same issues. However, this book focuses on commonalities among religious lobbyists that persist despite profound political disagreements. By concentrating on the similarities among religious lobbyists, more will be learned about the broader influence of religion in American politics. By identifying common characteristics among diverse groups of religious lobbyists, we begin to understand the common impact of religion—and nothing else—on their politics.

STUDYING THE WASHINGTON PROPHETS

Previous works on religious lobbying have provided some
answers to questions concerning the role of religion in
American politics, but they have been lacking in at least
two respects. First, existing studies have usually focused on
only one segment of the universe of organized religious interests, usually the activity of the religious right. They serve
as case studies that reveal much about particular parts of
religious political activism, but less about the broader significance of religion in general. Second, when research proj-
ects have moved beyond case studies to focus on the
breadth of religious political activism,[26] there has been neither a significant integration with the larger body of interest
group literature nor an explicit comparison with nonreligious groups. As a result, the distinctive character of religious political activism has been obscured. Finally, the
study of religion has not contributed significantly to the
broader development of theories of interest group politics.
There have been many descriptive studies of the behavior
of some organized religious interests, but no enduring con-
clusions about the distinctiveness of that behavior.

The major exception is Allen Hertzke's *Representing God
in Washington*. This book provides a rich interpretation that
focuses on the concept of representation. Hertzke's work
provides deep insights about the work of religious lobbyists, but he provides neither direct comparisons with nonreligious lobbyists nor a thorough integration into the tradition of interest group theory. Hertzke illumines the
different ways that religious lobbyists "represent God in
Washington." This book focuses more on common patterns
of behavior and the contrasts between religious and secular
lobbyists.

The unique behavior of religious lobbyists suggests the
need for revisions in theories of interest groups. Two major
theoretical traditions have explained lobbying: pluralism

and elitism. Pluralists argue that politics can best be understood by looking at the panoply of groups who bring their concerns to government. Everything else—institutions or individuals, for example—fails to illumine the crucial interactions of politics. Each group attempts to pressure government through the force of its campaign contributions, its members' votes, or the sheer force of its ideas. In response, government acts as a referee in this struggle and mediates a compromise among contending interests. The form of the compromise depends upon the relative amounts of pressure exerted by opposing groups. For example, business lobbyists seek a decrease in the minimum wage, while labor lobbyists seek an increase. The exact level of the minimum wage will vary according to the pressure generated by business and labor lobbyists.

Pluralism's weakness is that it lumps all lobbying strategies into the generic category of pressure; it is not able to discriminate among different kinds of pressure. Pluralists cannot explain why groups with different types of goals may adopt different strategies. Religious lobbyists generate pressure in the classic pluralist sense, but they have different expectations about the outcomes of their pressure politics. Pluralist theory provides an incisive explanation for lobbyists who have goals of incremental change and a willingness to compromise. But religious lobbyists seek fundamental change and are less willing to compromise. This kind of goal requires different strategies and generates different kinds of political pressure. As a result, more nuances are necessary to explain the full range of lobbying strategies.

At first glance, elite theory might provide a satisfactory alternative to pluralism. Elite theorists criticize pluralists because they ignore the ways in which latent groups are prevented from forming. Pluralists focus only on existing groups. Groups like migrant farm workers or the homeless clearly have grievances, but they have not organized fully.

While pluralists focus on the politics of bargaining, elite theorists try to explain why many never make it to the bargaining table in the first place. Elite theorists point to different forms of domination that suppress the interests of nonelites.

Because religious lobbyists have an antielitist or prophetic strategy, this body of theory might be more appropriate for this book. However, elite theorists seek primarily to explain the nature of elite domination, not the development of antielitist strategy. Some scholars look at parties,[27] the presidency,[28] and a reinvigorated rule of law[29] to counteract elite dominance; however, few critics of pluralism look at lobbying as an antielitist strategy. This book makes that attempt.

This book also analyzes the ways in which prophetic lobbyists relate to the members of their churches, synagogues, and organizations. To explain the internal politics of organizations, the most prominent explanation is exchange theory, in which a group leader supplies a benefit—either material, solidary, or purposive—in exchange for group membership. The exchange of benefits generates loyalty from members. Often people join an organization for reasons other than its lobbying activities. For example, laborers may join a labor union to gain higher wages (a material benefit); they may not have any interest in politics. Similarly, individuals may join a church or other religious organization to meet people with common concerns (a solidary benefit). If religious organizations lobby, it is because leaders have provided members with sufficient benefits to allow the leaders to get involved in politics. In the language of exchange theory, the leaders have generated a surplus through their provision of benefits. Exchange theorists focus on this exchange between leaders and members. By focusing only on the relationship between individuals, exchange theory has the virtue of parsimony. Yet, exchange explanations can be tautological. In the event of successful group maintenance, it is almost impossible not to find some evidence of benefit exchange. The empirical work suffers from a lack of clarity about the exact nature of the exchange.

In addition to its focus on interest group theory, this book will also contribute to the broader discussion of radical politics—both religious and nonreligious. In political science and elsewhere, few have studied groups that seek more fundamental change. Theodore Lowi states that political science has had difficulty in "dealing with political radicalism in U.S. history except as something exceptional, sporadic, and temporary. [Yet,] radical politics is as regular as mainstream, even if less frequent."[30] This book will build upon and utilize existing research in political science to appraise the radical politics of organized religious interests. This approach will enhance our understanding of both radical and religious politics.

But this text is more than a discussion of radical politics; it is about the articulation and organization of religious beliefs professed by an exceptionally large number of Americans. Not only does the United States lead the industrialized world in the numbers of members of religious organizations, it also boasts the greatest variety. No other country is more religiously diverse. The religious bodies are diverse in their theologies, political views, styles of worship, and the socioeconomic status of their members. They range from conservative fundamentalist Protestants to liberal mainline Protestants, from liturgical Roman Catholics to freewheeling spontaneous Pentecostals, and from wealthy believers to the faithful poor. Despite their dazzling diversity, there is also unity. Religious lobbyists share a common purpose and vision. That vision is nothing less than to bring America back to its deepest traditions. In order to fully comprehend the role of religion in American politics, we must understand both the unity and the diversity of religious faith.

DEFINING THE RELIGIOUS INTEREST

Little is known about the behavior of organized religious
interests in part because the term "religious interest" is
vague. The interests of other organizations like the National
Association of Manufacturers or the American Medical Association seem more clear because they consist of a distinct
group of people who agree on most of their political
agenda. Lobbyists for these organizations work for legislation that directly benefits the interests of business and doc-
tors. The task is more complex in the religious community
because of the dazzling variety of churches and synagogues
and the doubts about whether these religious organizations
should have lobbyists representing them at all. Members of
churches and synagogues can work for their political concerns through nonreligious organizations. Thus we must
ask whether religious organizations have politically relevant goals which constitute demands that can be made of
the political system. How can the concerns of religious citizens be translated into a political strategy in the nation's
capital?

Women face a similar dilemma. Many women claim a
need for lobbies to represent their gender. Yet others claim
that women are too diverse to be represented by a gender-
based lobby. Women's interests can be advocated by lobbyists for labor, business, or the civil rights community. In
response to this quandary, political scientist Virginia Sapiro
asked the question, "When are interests interesting?" That
is, when is an interest considered a viable and legitimate
entity in the political process? She answers that there is indeed a distinct women's interest; there are concerns that
affect only women, who need and seek representation.
Without a women's lobby, legislation concerning issues like
comparable worth, abortion, equal rights, and other labor
laws might be ignored. Furthermore, women are uniquely
affected by a range of policy issues that do not have

"women" in title or text. Issues of war, economics, and international politics also affect women differently. Without organizations to represent women, the interests and perspectives of women are diluted and even lost.[31]

A religious interest also constitutes a unique dimension of the U.S. political process. The uniqueness stems from the singular characteristics of religion that encourage political activism. Religion can be defined as (1) a social-cultural group, (2) a set of institutions, or (3) a creed or doctrine. As a social-cultural group or a set of institutions, the religious interest consists both of specific religious institutions and of the group of individuals who profess religious beliefs. As a doctrine, the religious interest is an ancient tradition of belief.[32] All three dimensions of religion make up the religious interest.[33]

Because religion is in part a social-cultural phenomenon, religious lobbyists must represent millions of citizens who are their members. For representatives of denominations such as the Episcopal or Methodist churches, these are the "persons in the pews." For leaders of membership organizations such as the Moral Majority, these are the dues-paying members. According to a recent Gallup poll, 68 percent of U.S. citizens said they were members of a religious organization,[34] most of whom are represented by lobbyists in Washington. No other category of organizations can claim such a sweeping membership. If fully engaged politically, religious organizations have the potential to completely dominate the policy process. For a number of reasons discussed more fully in other parts of this book, most religious organizations are reluctant to engage aggressively in the policy process. Nonetheless, religious lobbyists represent two-thirds of the American citizenry. Only the major political parties can rival their breadth of membership.

In addition to their members, religious lobbyists represent the tangible interests of churches and synagogues as institutions. These interests include schools, colleges, hospitals, nursing homes, charitable agencies, and life insurance companies. Religious lobbyists also defend the freedom of religious expression guaranteed in the First Amendment. This freedom is essential to the survival and growth of churches, synagogues, and other religious organizations in the United States. Without religious lobbyists, advocacy for religious liberty and religious institutions will not take place. Interestingly, religious lobbyists spend very little energy defending their institutional interests. But when such a defense is deemed necessary, lobbyists work fervently to defend encroachments on religious liberty. In the first session of the 103rd Congress (1993), religious lobbyists—both conservative and liberal—worked feverishly for the Religious Freedom Restoration Act. They viewed that legislation as essential to preserving religious liberty and warding off direct challenges to religious belief.[35] Previously, during debate about the Tax Reform Act of 1986, religious lobbyists worked to preserve the deduction for charitable gifts. In each of these cases, religious lobbyists were working for legislation that benefited the institutions of religion directly.

When religious lobbyists represent domestic constituencies and institutional concerns, they behave in ways that are strikingly similar to the actions of their secular counterparts. If these activities were the extent of the representation offered by religious lobbyists, there would be scant reason to understand religious lobbyists as distinctive. They could easily be categorized as public interest groups, and indeed, they often have been. Most studies of interest groups have placed religious interest groups in this very category.[36] Most scholars have failed to see the need for a separate category of religious groups.

They are mistaken because religious lobbyists are called to represent and remain faithful to a theological tradition in addition to representing institutions and members. The representation of this ancient heritage makes the religious interest distinctive. While all lobbyists must attend to the concerns of their members and institutions, religious lobbyists must remain faithful to the demands of a tradition of faith. This tradition is nothing less than a religious community's understanding of God's call. From religious texts and the discernment of members, lobbyists and religious leaders come to believe that they are called by God to specific forms of belief and action. Sometimes their allegiance to a religious tradition causes religious lobbyists to take positions that conflict with those of their members. Allegiance to theological truth is seen to be more important than a majority vote.

In the United States, religious lobbyists share a common Jewish and Christian heritage. All share common roots in the Hebrew Scriptures. All trace their origins in some way to Israel. There is, however, much diversity. Different religious traditions interpret the Scriptures differently. Catholic and Protestant traditions add the New Testament to their canon of sacred texts. Within each of the major traditions of faith, there is also much disagreement. Religious lobbyists disagree, often vehemently, on the political and ethical expressions of their religious faiths. Summarizing broadly, liberal religious lobbyists are riveted by questions of economic and social justice. Their sources of inspiration are the Old Testament prophets who call people of faith to "beat their swords into plowshares, their spears into pruning hooks"[37] and to "let justice roll down like waters, righteousness like an ever flowing stream."[38] In addition, these lobbyists recall Jesus' words in Luke: "The Spirit of the Lord is upon me, because he has anointed me to preach good news to the poor. . . . to set at liberty those who are oppressed."[39] This emphasis on peace and justice inspires lobbyists to call for deep cuts in military spending and increased government spending for the poor.

In contrast, conservative lobbyists focus more on issues of individual morality than on economic justice. They draw much of their theological support from the Pauline letters

of the New Testament in which there are many injunctions
to individual holiness and purity. With Scriptures like these
as their foundation, they oppose abortion rights, gay rights,
and the Equal Rights Amendment. They also are strong advocates of school prayer and often support increased defense spending. Conservatives feel that these policy positions are necessary to support traditional family structures
that are the backbone of traditional morality.

Although religious lobbies disagree on many policy issues, they share some common themes as well. Sociologist
Robert Wuthnow contends that "almost every issue since
the late 1960s that has animated the energies of religious
people has been associated with the feeling that the power
of government was too great."[40] For example, the liberals
who protested the Vietnam War and the conservatives who
opposed the racial integration of American society both
drew their energy from the belief that government was ex-
ercising excessive power. In the 1980 elections, Wuthnow
states,

> active church-goers were much more likely to become
> politically involved than less active church-goers—but only
> if they thought government was becoming too
> powerful. . . . Even religious conservatives, who according
> to their more liberal detractors would wish to see a
> government-imposed form of totalitarian morality, are
> likely in their rhetoric to define their objectives more in
> terms of restraining the hand of government than of
> courting its power.[41]

Several additional examples illustrate this common antip-
athy toward government. Religious liberals, who often call
for an expanded welfare state, are among the few voices
protesting against workfare provisions in welfare reform
legislation because those requirements entail too much government intrusion into peoples' lives.[42] In the 1988 presidential campaign, the supporters of both Jesse Jackson and Pat
Robertson agreed that government was elitist. Poll data

show that supporters of both these candidates were far more likely than the supporters of both Bush and Dukakis to view government as "pretty much run by a few big interests . . . [rather than] for the benefit of all people." Though Jackson and Robertson are on opposite ends of the political spectrum, their followers share common concerns about the overbearing power of government.[43]

THE DATA SET

Beyond defining the religious interest,[44] representatives of the religious interest must be located.[45] Though they could be referred to as religious interest groups, I use the term "organized religious interests" in order to create a broader analytical category than traditional understandings of interest groups. The term "interest group" refers to membership organizations, but the term "organized interest" refers to membership organizations, coalitions of membership organizations, and large denominations such as the Presbyterian Church. Schlozman and Tierney have pioneered the use of the term "organized interest,"[46] and this book follows their lead and adapts their terminology. The broader term is especially important when discussing organizations like religious denominations that contain structural characteristics of both institutions and membership groups.

To identify organized religious interests, an operational definition is necessary. Political scientist Paul J. Weber and journalist T. L. Stanley state:

> By religious interest groups we mean groups which are active in national politics and which identify themselves as religious, have a largely religious membership, and/or are active in areas traditionally considered to be of significance to religious groups, including but not limited to classic church-state issues. By active in national politics is meant groups which attempt to influence, directly or indirectly by

some positive, material means, the content and direction of one or more national public policies.[47]

Using this definition, Weber and Stanley identified 74 religious interest groups in Washington, D.C., in 1980. In the early 1990s, Weber and W. Landis Jones searched for all religious interest groups in the United States.[48] They identified 120 groups that focus on national policy. My definition is narrower in several ways; as a result, I locate fewer religious interests than they do. Weber, Stanley, and Jones include groups such as the American Ethical Union and the American Civil Liberties Union that are nominally non-religious but are active on issues of great concern to religion. In contrast, the groups in this study are limited to those that are explicitly religious and are located in the Washington, D.C., area.

In addition, Weber and Jones list some groups that do very little lobbying. Included in their profiles are such Washington-based organizations as the Center of Concern and the Institute on Religion and Democracy. These organizations are primarily educational organizations; lobbying the national government is a low priority. While judgments in this area are difficult and complicated by lobbying laws, the groups in this book are religious organizations whose *primary* purpose is to lobby national government and influence national public policies. This definition means that the groups and institutions must show a belief in a power that transcends this world and have a goal of influencing national public policies as their *primary* purpose.[49]

A BRIEF OVERVIEW

Chapter 2 sketches a brief history of religious lobbying. Different patterns of church-state relations in the United States are outlined. In American history, religion has provided both legitimation and criticism of the actions of the state.

Religion legitimizes the state through actions such as Billy Graham's frequent visits to several presidents. These visits constituted blessings of presidential policy. A recent example during the presidency of George Bush was Graham's overnight stay in the White House on the eve of the Persian Gulf War. In contrast to Graham's consecration of the state, religion criticizes the state when it protests the state's policies. Though religion has both a legitimating and critical function, the evidence shows that contemporary religious lobbyists serve primarily a critical function. By pointing to other patterns in history, we can better understand contemporary religious activism.

Chapter 3 develops the theory of religious lobbying. The new theory builds upon existing theories—pluralism, elitism, and exchange theory—that have been used by other scholars to explain lobbying. After describing existing theories, a revision is proposed. Chapter 4 describes the universe of groups in this study in more detail. The membership, financial resources, political ideologies, and theological beliefs of religious lobbyists are assessed.

Chapter 5 offers evidence that reveals the prophetic perspective of religious lobbyists. A series of interviews of religious lobbyists are the primary data. Through these interviews, religious lobbyists express their prophetic outlook in their own words. Chapter 6 goes on to compare and contrast the specific tactics of religious and nonreligious lobbyists. Some distinct patterns emerge. Chapter 7 explores the internal political processes—the relationship between leaders and members—of organized religious interests. It develops an explanation of agreements and disagreements between leaders and members. Chapter 8 concludes with an argument in favor of religious lobbying and comments on directions for future research.

2
CHAPTER

Prophetic Religious Lobbying and the History of Church-State Relations

The prophetic religious lobbying of the late twentieth century offers both continuities and contrasts with the religious political activism of past eras. Rejecting a prophetic perspective, organized religion has sometimes ignored public life entirely and created a privatistic retreat. Understood this way, religion is a private matter of individual faith. Contemporary religious lobbyists reject this role, but others argue that it is the appropriate role for religion. Because many Americans believe that religion should be a private affair, this view influences the context of religious lobbying. Religious lobbyists must constantly defend their very presence in the political arena.

At the other extreme, organized religion sometimes has served to legitimate the state with a priestly blessing of public policies. When organized religion fills a legitimating role, its relationship with the state is cozier and closer than the relationship of contemprary religious lobbyists. Its primary function is to offer religious sanction—not prophetic criticism—to the nation's public policies. A look at past eras when religion and the state were more closely intertwined is very relevant to understanding the religious lobbying of today. Since religious lobbyists seek a closer alignment between religious values and the public policies of the state,

assessing past eras when the connection between religion
and politics was closer can help us understand the vision of
religious lobbyists.

THE EXPLICIT MERGER OF RELIGION AND THE
STATE IN COLONIAL AMERICA

In the history of Western nations, the most pronounced example of the merger of religion and the state was medieval
Europe. "Medieval society . . . was a religious society dominated by a Christian world view and deeply influenced by
a bureaucratic universal church. In this society, individuals
were not given the choice of whether they wanted to have
religion. They must have it."[1] Political citizenship in this society was often dependent on church membership. With
some exceptions, the church reigned supreme over the
state. According to Ernst Troeltsch, "Medieval society can
be regarded as the institutional articulation of a relatively
unified Christian culture embodied in both the universal
church and the empire."[2]

Although the fusion of church and state was in some tension throughout the medieval era, the Reformation was the
beginning of the end of this relationship between church
and state. As a part of his protest against the Roman Catholic Church, Martin Luther argued that Scripture, not the
church tradition or hierarchy, was authoritative for theological questions. Concerning politics, Luther clearly felt
that religious faith had political implications; however, he
argued further that organized religion should not have a
privileged position on political issues. In the affairs of state,
reason was the guiding force. And reason was accessible to
believers and nonbelievers alike. This view began to sever
the cords intertwining church and state.

Other reformers worked for a closer relationship between church and state. The religious commonwealth that

John Calvin established in Geneva is one example.[3] Though part of the Reformation himself, Calvin saw a closer connection between religion, morality, and politics than did Martin Luther. Since most church members in eighteenth- and nineteenth-century America were descendants either of Calvin or of the Church of England, America featured established state churches until the beginning of the nineteenth century. Often church and state were so intertwined that the state received a kind of theological and ecclesiastical sanction in order to govern. Public policies often bore the clear imprint of religious influence. Reminiscent of medieval Europe, the state sometimes used a variety of coercive measures to maintain the allegiance of its citizens to the church.

In very different ways, Massachusetts and Pennsylvania were the most prominent example of this close relationship between church and state in colonial America. In Massachusetts, the Puritans sought to establish a Puritan commonwealth. They desired a community with civil and ecclesiastical laws that were derived from Christian principles of morality and justice. Evidence of these beliefs is found in the speeches and sermons of John Winthrop, Puritan leader and first governor of what is now Massachusetts. Just before their landing in 1630, Winthrop gave a sermon entitled "A Model of Christian Charity." He said,

> We are a Company professing ourselves fellow members of Christ through a special overruling providence . . . to set up in the wilderness a due form of Government both civil and ecclesiastical. We have entered into a Covenant with Him [God] for his work, and we have taken out a commission. God permitted us to draw our own Articles and we have signed the contract by essaying the venture. If we land safely in Massachusetts that will be God's signature on the contract; that is, we shall know that we have correctly interpreted His will in the signs of the times, and thenceforth we shall be irrevocably bound in this relation with the Deity.[4]

Drawing from the New Testament book of Matthew, the Puritans painted a vision of a "city on a hill" that all nations could emulate. As governor, Winthrop made clear the ethical and moral principles for political and social life in this new community.

> We must delight in each other, make other's conditions our own, rejoyce together, mourn together, labor and suffer together, always having before our eyes our commission and community in the work, our community as members of the same body. . . . We shall find that the God of Israel is among us, when ten of us shall be able to resist a thousand of our enemies, when He shall make us a praise and glory, that men shall say of succeeding plantations; "The Lord make it like that of New England.[5]

Though religious principles permeated the Puritan commonwealth, the relationship between church and state was not as overlapping as in the Middle Ages. Massachusetts was not a theocracy. Church officials in no sense governed the colony; instead, citizens elected public officials. However, church membership was initially a precondition for citizenship. Five years after the founding of the Massachusetts Bay Colony in 1630, a "rule was established that only professed and examined saints, who proved by public confession in church that the saving faith had come to them, could become full communicants of the church and voting citizens of the state."[6]

Church and state were not directly fused, but the connections remained powerful. If we understand the state more broadly than as a collection of elected and appointed officials, the connection between church and state is especially strong. Offering a broader interpretation, political scientist Theda Skocpol suggests that "states may be viewed more macroscopically as configurations of organization and action that influence the meanings and methods of politics for all groups and classes in society."[7] Understood this way, the fusion of church and state in Puritan America is more evident. While the church did not directly control the state, governance took place by consent of Puritan citizens and in accordance with the principles of Puritan Christianity.

While the Puritans made laws grounded in their religious values, it is clear that those values did not include tolerance. Sydney Ahlstrom wrote that "Puritans were insufferable, self-righteous precisionists with narrow minds and blue noses, authoritarian, clericalists, intolerant, and anti-democratic."[8] Because of their intolerance, many who disagreed with the Puritan way fled Massachusetts and found refuge in other colonies. The most prominent victims of Puritan persecution were three individuals who were banished from Massachusetts Bay and moved on to found the colony of Rhode Island. The three were Roger Williams, Samuel Gorton, and the first woman to play a prominent role in American church history, Anne Hutchinson.

Differing from Massachusetts, the colony of Pennsylvania was a more tolerant version of a religiously inspired state. Pennsylvania was founded by William Penn, an English Quaker, who received a huge tract of land from King Charles II as a repayment of a debt owed to Penn's father, who was an English vice admiral. Penn used the land to invite European Quakers to come to America and undertake a holy experiment.[9] Like Massachusetts, church and state were intertwined in that new society. Penn stated in 1682 that "government seems to me a part of religion itself, a thing sacred in its institution and end."[10] With this foundation, religiously inspired laws were passed. Because of Biblical injunctions forbidding adultery, one Pennsylvania law decreed that adulterers "for the first offense be publicly whipt and suffer one whole year's imprisonment in the House of Correction at hard labor" and for any additional infraction the punishment would be "imprisonment in manner aforesaid During Life."[11] Another set of laws provided for the fair treatment of the Indians[12] and the education of Negroes.[13]

Although the Quakers were to dominate Pennsylvanian culture, they—unlike the leaders of Massachusetts—affirmed the principles of religious liberty. Most interpreters say that it was their own experience of religious persecution in England that led them to grant this freedom in Pennsylvania. Although religious liberty was affirmed, the Quakers and their values enveloped the political process. They affirmed religious pluralism, but nevertheless they dominated the colonial assembly and attempted to write legislation that was consistent with Quaker beliefs. In the end, this paradox could not endure. Pennsylvania declined as a Quaker state in part because the guarantees of religious liberty attracted a wide diversity of non-Quakers. These new groups included Presbyterians, Lutherans, Methodists, Catholics, and Baptists.

Specifically, the Quakers' commitment to pacifism conflicted with the need of states to participate in wars. For some time the Quakers managed an uneasy truce and continued to appropriate funds that indirectly paid for England's wars.[14] However, when the colony was in an actual war with the Delaware and Shawnee Indians, the tension proved unresolvable. Because of the demands of their faith, the Quakers resigned as a group from the colonial assembly and withdrew from active political participation in government. They would never dominate the religious assembly again; however, their institutionalization of religious liberty endured.

Puritan Massachusetts and Quaker Pennsylvania are examples of two different American versions of close relationships between church and state. When church and state are so inextricably intertwined, religion usually does not provide a prophetic critique of the state. Because organized religion is part of the state, it is able to influence public policy more directly. Consequently, religious organizations engage in a more mainstream style of politics. Religious leaders have a close relationship with public officials; indeed, most public officials are lay members of the dominant faith. With such a deep religious imprint on public policies, there is no need for the dominant church to seek fundamental change and consequently a lesser need for the kind of prophetic lobbying that is the central strategy of contemporary religious lobbyists. Because many religious lobbyists in the late twentieth century seek a closer relationship between their religious values and the policies of the state, these past eras are relevant for understanding contemporary religious lobbying. Past periods in which church and state were more closely intertwined provide glimpses of religious lobbyists' vision for the future of American politics.

EXPLICIT SEPARATION OF CHURCH AND STATE IN THE UNITED STATES: THE FOUNDING PERIOD

With many different forms of religion taking root in American soil, problems arose between churches. Because most religions claimed to be the one true church, it was difficult for believers to accept the legitimacy of other churches. In nine colonies, the predominant churches were officially established as state churches. In Massachusetts, it was the Puritans. In Virginia, it was the Anglicans. Because of the intolerance of many of those churches, the coexistence of different religions often proved as difficult in the new world as in the old. The unorthodox were often persecuted or banished for their beliefs.

The most famous victim of religious persecution was Roger Williams. Williams founded the colony of Rhode Island in large part because the Puritan establishment of Massachusetts banished him from the Bay Colony. In 1636, Williams and a band of followers established the community of Providence. Like Winthrop and his followers in Massachusetts, they tried to make laws that conformed to their religious belief, but, unlike the Massachusetts Puritans, they allowed complete freedom of worship. Rhode Island worked to base civil laws on the second tablet of the Ten Commandments, but permitted complete religious liberty in the observance and interpretation of the first tablet. The commandments of the first tablet deal with the fundamental definitions of God and faith while the second tablet deals with issues involving behavior in community, such as adultery, theft, and covetousness. Williams and his comrades deemed this latter group of topics to be legitimate concerns of the state; the former were matters of individual conscience only.[15]

In Rhode Island, different forms of belief were possible. Many were not thrilled with the results of the Rhode Island experiment. New England cleric Cotton Mather complained that Rhode Island was home to "Antinomians, Familists, Anabaptists, AntiSabbatarians, Arminians, Socinians, Quakers, Ranters, every thing in the World but Roman Catholicks, and Real Christians."[16] Although this statement illustrates deep antagonism toward the idea of religious liberty, the guarantee of religious liberty has distinguished the colony of Rhode Island in American history.

Influenced only slightly by Rhode Island, the founders of the United States moved toward disestablishing religion and guaranteeing religious liberty.[17] The United States became the first Western country since Emperor Constantine became a Christian to separate church and state so sharply. Instead of one officially established church providing one vision, the legitimacy of many different churches was granted. As a result, the founders intended, and to a large degree achieved, a religious pluralism that is unique in world history.[18] No other country has had so many differing religions.[19] Though established churches at the state level would last almost another half century, one organized religion would never dominate the national government.

But while separating the institutions of church and state, the founders maintained that religion was essential for the

governance of the new republic. Though the founders varied tremendously in their personal beliefs, they all were
convinced of the importance of religion as a necessary support for republican government. Benjamin Franklin declared that most people "have need of the motives of religion to restrain them from vice, to support their virtue, and
retain them in the practice of it till it becomes habitual."
George Washington constantly invoked God to support the
war effort. In his farewell address in 1796, he stated that
"religion and morality are indispensable supports to political prosperity." John Adams insisted that "it is Religion and
Morality alone which can establish the principles upon
which Freedom can securely stand. A patriot must be a religious man."[20]

Although they agreed that religion must provide a unifying infusion of morals, the founders disagreed on the ap-
propriateness of other kinds of political behavior by organized religions. In the Constitution, the only mention of
organized religion was the prohibition against religious
litmus tests for public officials. Clearly there was some concern. At one point Thomas Jefferson advocated a ban on the
holding of public office by the clergy. He stated that organized religion should refrain from politics because of the
authoritarian tendencies of religion. Jefferson argued that
there is a "wall of separation" between the institutional
church and state. Though the wall metaphor was originally
used in a somewhat casual way by Jefferson in a letter to
the Baptist Association of Danbury, Connecticut, subsequent legal reasoning and public discourse have referred to
the metaphor as if it were part of the constitution itself.[21]
The vision of the metaphor is of two institutions separated
by an impenetrable wall; the resulting controversy is that
some people have allegiances to both institutions. State and
society must decide how a group defined by religion can
act on the other side of the wall.

James Madison was less strict than Jefferson and called

for a "line of separation." The metaphor of a "line" rather
than a "wall" allows for some interaction between church
and state. Yet Madison feared that state churches would
tend to promote "superstition, bigotry and persecution."[22]
Madison worried that one religion could become predominant and threaten the nation's liberty. To cure the ill effects
of religious factions, Madison argued that a "multiplicity of
sects" was the best guarantor of liberty. Consistent with the
broader logic of *The Federalist*, No. 10, he believed that the
existence of opposing sects would prevent tyranny. He
stated, "A religious sect may degenerate into a political faction in a part of the Confederacy; but the variety of sects
dispersed over the entire face of it must secure the national
councils against any danger from that source."[23] Madison
sought the disestablishment of religion because it fostered
the formation of many different religions.

The founders seemed to be moving in two directions
with regard to religion. First, they wanted to encourage religion by guaranteeing the right of religious expression.
They welcomed the influence of religion in society. But,
they also wanted to guard against religious dominance.
They did so by refusing to establish a state church and by
encouraging the multiplicity of opposing groups that would
balance each other and lead to social stability. For their
part, representatives of organized religion also had conflicting views. Recognizing the multiplicity of other religions,
individual churches and groups were threatened by the
possibility that an established church would oppose their
beliefs and even persecute them. Fueled by this fear, many
religious leaders favored the separation of church and state.
But in the tradition of Winthrop and Penn, many sought to
shape a society in which all laws were based on one's religious faith. That concern kept religious people and organizations deeply involved in American public life.

These paradoxical concerns have endured to the present.
As a result, there are contradictory expectations regarding

the appropriate role for the variety of organized religions in American public life. Even as they practice their own faith, most Americans support some restrictions on the political activity of organized religion. Poll data show that most Americans would not vote for an atheist for president, yet the same poll shows that few Americans support the active involvement of organized religion in politics.[24] This result is consistent with both the founders' support of individual-level religious beliefs and their fears of organized religion as a political force. In this context, organized religion has responded in a number of ways; the remainder of the chapter identifies three forms of response.

PRIVATE RELIGION AND THE WITHDRAWAL FROM PUBLIC LIFE

With their religious liberty protected, many religious communities seek to withdraw from public life and to exist completely apart from the state. Even though they desire distance from the state, religious people affirm the state's guarantee of religious liberty. They are thankful that the state has not designated an established religion because they realize that their religion might not be the national faith. Indeed, they could be persecuted. This affirmation of religious liberty often leads to the support of other actions of the state: Religion rarely criticizes the state that grants religious freedom.

A conservative variant of Lutheran theology features this privatized faith. Lutherans of this stripe have often resisted direct political activism. The primary responsibility for the church was to work to encourage faithful relationships between individuals and God. In politics, the church has no privileged insight. Martin Luther himself was reported to have once said that "he would rather be ruled by a smart Turk than a dumb Christian." Because of this tradition, Lutheran church bodies, and often individual Lutherans, have sometimes avoided political involvement.[25] One Lutheran response to slavery illustrates this tendency. Sydney Ahlstrom notes, "The Lutheran Synods organized by new immigrant groups were for the most part in free territory, and they tended to oppose slavery, though they naturally preferred not to commit the church on what they regarded as secular political issues."[26] In this sense, faith and politics are connected. Religious faith was seen as incompatible with slavery, but religious citizens avoided staking out a "church" position on the issue. The church instead pledged obedience to the governing authorities.

More extreme than these Lutherans, fundamentalist Christians have traditionally seen religion as an even more private matter. Until recently, fundamentalists have had little interest in politics. Their primary concern was the private relationship between individuals and God.[27] An early fundamentalist theologian, I. M. Haldeman, wrote that attempts at political and social change were "like cleaning and decorating the staterooms of a sinking ship."[28] As late as 1965, Jerry Falwell stated,

> We have few ties to this earth. We pay our taxes, cast our votes as a responsibility of citizenship, obey the laws of the land, and do other things demanded of us by the society in which we live. But at the same time, we are cognizant that our only purpose on this earth is to know Christ and to make Him known.[29]

Obviously, there were significant changes in this view in the late 1970s and early 1980s. Fundamentalists cast off their earlier reluctance about political involvement and created one of the more powerful political movements of the late twentieth century. Republican leaders, including Presidents Reagan and Bush, courted the movement and brought its members into the Republican party.

In the 1990s, however, some fundamentalist organizations folded or left Washington, D.C. The most prominent fundamentalist leader of the 1980s, Jerry Falwell, withdrew from Washington and dissolved the two organizations that he had founded. The latter half of the eighties saw the death of several other conservative Christian organizations including the National Christian Action Coalition, the American Coalition for Traditional Values, and the Freedom Council.[30] While fundamentalist Christians remain extremely active in national as well as state and local politics, the dissolution of many groups is perhaps evidence that some —not all—are reverting to the privatistic beliefs they held earlier.

Other religious groups have also tended toward this position. At a minimum, most churches and synagogues keep their central focus on worship. Political activity is secondary to religion's first priority of prayer and devotion. The reluctance to engage in political affairs is rooted in the fear that political involvement has the potential to diminish the power and purity of religious belief. Many believers feel that political involvement will transform churches and synagogues into purely political organizations. Because of this belief, they avoid politics.

Ironically, this private role of religion sometimes results in a religious sanction of the state. If there is no explicit criticism of government, then a common inference is that organized religion is supportive. Moreover, a government that provides freedom to worship must be granted obedience and support. This sanction is even justified by scriptural passages that state, "Everyone must submit himself to the governing authorities, for there is no authority except that which God has established. The authorities that exist have been established by God."[31] Interpreting this text as a call to obedience, there is an implicit fusion of church and state that is similar to the situation in colonial America discussed previously.

More support comes from interpretations of Martin Lu-

ther, who in the sixteenth century admonished his fol
lowers to obey the state in all matters—unless the state
infringed on religious liberty. As long as the freedom of
worship is provided, politics is inconsequential to the institutional church.[32] As a result, if religious liberty is guaranteed, then religious leaders should support government.
Going one step further, some leaders argue that religious
faith thrives best under a democratic government. They
then adamantly oppose anything that might threaten de
mocracy. Sometimes their defense of democracy and religious liberty leads to deeper political involvements as they
express support for an anticommunist foreign policy and a
criticism of the welfare state as "creeping socialism."

Theologian Richard John Neuhaus is a contemporary ad-
herent of this position. He states:

> Christians may see in democracy a development under
> divine guidance. Democracy is the appropriate form of
> governance in a fallen creation in which no person or
> institution, including the church, can infallibly speak for
> God. Democracy is the necessary expression of humility in
> which all persons and institutions are held accountable to
> transcendent purpose imperfectly discerned.[33]

Demonstrating his commitment in the 1980s, he helped
found and run the Institute for Religion and Democracy.
The purpose of the organization is to "revitalize the link
between Christian faith and democratic values and to expand religious liberty, the cornerstone of all other human
rights."[34] Such advocacy led Neuhaus and the IRD to support Reagan policy in Nicaragua and to challenge mainline
Protestant churches that did not support that policy. Neuhaus was critical of the political involvement of some religious organizations; in response, he sought to shape his
own form of political engagement.

Unlike Neuhaus, some religious individuals and groups
do seek a purely private religious experience. H. Richard
Niebuhr described one version of this private faith as

"Christ against culture."[35] Various types of monastic communities capture the counter-cultural spirit of this type. Yet others who advocate a more private faith also want religion to endorse the state as it promotes values and causes that are consistent with the demands of faith against culture.

PRIESTLY CIVIL RELIGION: THE BLESSING OF GOVERNMENT

Civil religion transforms the citizen's relationship to the state into a devotion to a higher power, something greater than the individual. Disciples of civil religion understand politics in religious terms.[36] While not necessarily supplanting belief in God, this veneration of the state intensifies the patriotism of citizens. Clearly, it diminishes the depth of criticism of the state. Ken Wald states, "So long as the nation conducts its affairs according to some higher purpose, it warrants allegiance from its citizens on grounds other than mere self-interest."[37]

This idea of civil religion has deep roots. Benjamin Franklin expressed it when he called for a religion of the republic, or a "publick religion." Franklin was arguing for a national or civil religion. According to Franklin, this civil religion was to exist separately from and in addition to the diversity of faiths of citizens. Franklin argued that varying forms of faith should lead to a common moral unity, "the essentials of every religion."[38] This moral unity would form the moral and spiritual foundation for democracy.[39]

Presidential speeches and actions provide evidence of this civil religion. Virtually every inaugural address—from Washington to Clinton—has included references to God or a Supreme Being.[40] When presidents make these references, they are acting as the high priest of American civil religion. Exhortations that America is the "New Israel" or a "chosen

people" are particularly vivid mixings of religious and political symbols. Similarly, the presidential contention that
God is active in public affairs also underscores the civil religion of the American republic. Most recently, Presidents
Ronald Reagan and Bill Clinton have used this kind of rhetoric. Typifying themes of his speeches, Ronald Reagan said,
"I have always believed that this land was placed here . . .
by some divine plan . . . to be found by a special kind of
people." He also repeatedly referred to America as "a shining city on a hill" with the potential to "begin the world
over again."[41] Similarly, Bill Clinton talks of establishing a
"New Covenant" with the American people.[42]

While presidential speeches serve as the sermons of
American civil religion, there are many civic rituals that
function as its liturgy. For many years, schoolchildren began their day in organized spoken prayer. Many still begin
by reciting a pledge of allegiance to "one nation under
God." Legislatures still open each day with prayer. Presidents take their oath of office on the Bible. The Supreme
Court opens its session with a bailiff stating, "God bless this
honorable court." Certain shrines like the Lincoln and Jefferson memorials function as civic temples. Some national
holidays like the Fourth of July, Memorial Day, and
Thanksgiving have a religious character to them. The holi-
day activities of civic parades, the raising of the flag, the
honoring of those who died in wars, and Thanksgiving
proclamations all add to the sacred ambience.

Organized religion can contribute to inculcating individuals with this civil religion.[43] One example is the placement
of flags near or on the altar of many Protestant and Catholic
churches.[44] During World War II, a V for victory was placed
on many church altars. When national symbols are inte-
grated into places of worship, the worship of God and nation are often intertwined. Religion is then deeply involved
in the political process, but the path of influence is less direct. Political influence occurs not through organizational

lobbying, but through shaping the way individuals interpret the political world. When individuals interpret the nation as a higher power worthy of their devotion, it can be very beneficial for the government. If the president becomes one's priest, then it is more difficult to criticize the president. In this way, organized religion serves to legitimate and support the state. Instead of challenging government, religion serves to support the policies of the government by giving them a kind of divine sanction. Though the connection is less direct than it is under theocratic regimes, church and state are again merged even in the context of institutional separation.

PROPHETIC CIVIL RELIGION: THE PERSPECTIVE OF CONTEMPORARY LOBBYISTS

Scholars of religion and politics note that today American civil religion is deeply divided. Religious lobbyists are advocating alternative civil religions.

> Like the religion found more generally in the nation's churches, it does not speak with a single voice, uniting the majority of Americans around common ideals. It has instead become a confusion of tongues speaking from different traditions and offering different visions of what America can and should be. Religious conservatives and liberals offer competing versions of American civil religion that seem to have very little of substance in common.[45]

In this situation, the contradictory visions of American society serve as a prophetic criticism of the status quo. Many still view politics in religious terms, but rather than approval, civil religion brings forth prophetic condemnation. Rather than calling people to deeper devotion to their government, religion calls people to more intense criticisms. Instead of connecting religious symbols to the state, the contradiction between religious values and the state's policies

is made manifest. Contemporary religious lobbyists proclaim this prophetic message.

Religion's angry voice has been heard repeatedly in
American history. Often the voice has fallen on deaf ears;
such is the vocation of prophecy. Yet at other times, the
prophetic voice of religion has resulted in epochal shifts in
the nation's direction. Several movements serve as the ar-
chetypes of religious prophecy in American public life. In
each instance, core values of the status quo were challenged. When Quakers and other religious groups began
the abolitionist movement, they were challenging the morality of a central economic institution: slavery. The abolitionist movement was not solely a religious movement, but
Quaker and African-American churches provided the critical mass of the movement.

In the abolitionist movement, African-American leaders
like Frederick Douglass understood their struggle for freedom in religious terms; it was their exodus. Like the ancient
Israelites enslaved by the Egyptian pharaoh, African-Americans were also in bondage. Consistent with prophetic
speech, Douglass criticized the oppressive status quo and
provided a vision of the Promised Land. After Douglass es-
caped from slavery, he thundered a cry for the abolition of
slavery and urged the whole country to deliverance. Douglass condemned slavery as sinful and threatened America
with God's just wrath. But Douglass also ended his prophetic condemnations with words of hope. "In jeremiah
fashion, Douglass denounced the multiplying present evils
but drew on the nation's sacred promise to announce his
undying faith in the eventual liberation of Afro-Americans
and, through it, the realization of America's democratic
mission."[46]

The prohibition movement is another example of religion's prophetic call for moral reform. Led by the Anti-Sa-
loon League, that movement mobilized millions and remained a major force in American politics for more than

two decades. The movement drew its major strength from churches. Denominational leaders held prominent positions in the organization. Furthermore, groups such as the Women's Christian Temperance Union were close allies. Some might refrain from calling the prohibition movement prophetic; however, the movement was usually linked to other progressive causes. Most prohibitionists also supported populist and progressive proposals for economic justice.

Like the abolitionist movement a century before it, the civil rights movement of the 1960s featured a prophetic religion. Fueled by the black church, the movement articulated its indignant protest using hymns and sermons. Political action in the form of civil disobedience led African-Americans to their exodus of freedom. Without the black church, the movement would have drowned under Bull Connor's hoses. In addition, the involvement of leaders of mostly white mainline denominations contributed much to the movement's success. Joseph Rauh, himself a participant in the civil rights movement, highlighted the role of white church leaders with this reflection:

> Standing outside the Committee Room was the most beautiful sight I had ever seen—twenty Episcopal priests, fully garbed, all young beautiful WASPs. I used to think that the only two people out in front for civil rights were a Negro and a Jew—Mitchell and myself. But this was something the committee members had never seen before. I knew then we really were in business. Indeed, I had the feeling that as the committee members filed past the priests into the Committee Room that they were going through a cheering section the way a football team runs out on the field through a band formation. It was a thrilling sight and dramatic evidence of the church's activity.[47]

In addition to the civil rights movement, the furious protest against U.S. involvement in Vietnam also drew much support from organized religion. Martin Luther King, Jr., against the advice of many who said it would hurt the struggle for civil rights, lent considerable effort to opposing the war. Other prominent religious leaders who opposed the Vietnam War included William Sloane Coffin, Jr., pastor of Riverside Church; Daniel and Philip Berrigan, both Catholic priests; and the well-known Rabbi Abraham Heschel. Clergy and Laity Concerned was a major religious organization formed to oppose the war. Many other religious leaders and organizations followed. Religious groups may not have formed the bulk of the antiwar movement, but, as sociologists Robert Bellah and Phillip Hammond argue, "the religious opposition to the Vietnam War was certainly more effective than the opposition of those who spelled America with a 'k.'"[48] Those who spelled America with a *k* were seen by the broader public as anarchistic protestors who sought to destroy the United States. Religious protestors, because they were rooted in an ancient tradition to which most Americans belonged, were able to articulate a more persuasive protest. The connection between religious symbols and antiwar protest added credibility to the movement.

In the 1980s and 1990s, conservative religious activists have promoted prophetic politics more vigorously than their liberal counterparts. Most notably, they decried the Washington establishment for its immorality and lack of concern for family values. In a book entitled *The Christian Right and Congress*, Matthew Moen concluded that, although fundamentalist Christians had only limited success in actually changing public policy outcomes, they were extremely successful at transforming the political agenda. Because of the Christian right, liberal interests were on the defensive for most of the 1980s.[49] Much legislative time was spent debating issues like school prayer and abortion. In both cases the Christian right was working to challenge the policies that it deemed inconsistent with religious faith and morality. Though the Christian right has yet to live up to its early billing as a force capable of taking over the government, it has taken over some state and local Republican parties, and it played a crucial role in the national Republican gains in the elections of November 1994.[50]

At the end of a tradition of religious political activism that includes the abolitionist, prohibitionist, civil rights, and Christian conservative movements, contemporary religious lobbyists protest the policies of the state. The broad-ranging and idealistic visions of contemporary religious lobbyists provide a fundamental challenge to the contemporary status quo. By attaching their faith to a policy agenda, religious lobbyists confront and contest the political establishment. They construct a prophetic civil religion which serves as a challenge to the civil religion that prevails in much of society at large.

Sociologist Robert Wuthnow states that there are two basic types of prophetic civil religions today: a conservative version and a liberal version.[51] For conservatives, government has a divinely ordained duty. The United States of America has a divinely sanctioned place in the world order. According to Jerry Falwell, the United States "is not a perfect nation, but it is without doubt the greatest and most influential nation in the world."[52] Conservatives are haunted by the belief that America is slipping away from this distinctive status. They have entered the political process to help preserve traditional morality. According to conservative Christians, an increased welfare state, the Equal Rights Amendment, gay rights, abortion rights, and perceived softness toward communism are all threats to the divinely sanctioned place of the United States. Their political efforts are an effort to transform the political agenda so that the United States can rightfully stand within this heavenly inspired vision.

Liberal religious activists agree that religion and politics are powerfully connected. Like their conservative counterparts, they seek a politics permeated by religious morality. However, their analysis of the role of America as a nation is very different from the conservatives' view.

> Liberals start from an entirely different place. The liberal version of American civil religion . . . focuses less on the nation as such, and more on humanity in general. According to this interpretation, America has a role to play in world affairs, not because it is a chosen people, but because it has vast resources at its disposal and because it has caused many of the problems currently facing the world. . . . liberal civil religion is much more likely to include arguments about basic human rights and common human problems. Issues like nuclear disarmament, human rights, world hunger, peace, and justice tend to receive special emphasis.[53]

In more theological terms, liberal activists participate in a long religious tradition of prophetic protest. Sociologist Donald E. Miller explains how religious leaders have understood their work:

> These persons will attempt to abolish idolatry in their midst. . . . They will follow in the tradition of the Hebrew prophets: feeding the poor, caring for widows and orphans, attacking economic systems that produce injustice. They will constitute a true community: unselfishly concerned for each others' needs and rejoicing in a love freely expressed.[54]

The pastoral letters of the National Conference of Catholic Bishops on nuclear war and the U.S. economy, written in the mid-1980s, are examples of this approach. In these letters, the bishops challenged the priorities of U.S. defense and economic policy. The peace letter specifically criticized the enormous levels of defense spending. In the letter on the economy, the bishops argued that the criteria for economic policy are the consequences for the entire community—particularly the poor. "Central to the biblical presentation of justice is that the justice of a community is measured by its treatment of the powerless in society."[55] Later in the letter, the bishops proposed a number of specific policies including the guarantee of jobs and a minimum level of income for all Americans.[56]

Religious organizations offer an alternative vision of society because of their religious roots. The language of religious texts reveals the source of their insurgent challenge. Consistently in the New Testament, Jesus told his followers that those who seek to save their lives will lose them, and those who lose their lives for the sake of the Gospel will save them.[57] The New Testament also commends a special concern for the poor and warnings to the rich.[58] Similarly, the Hebrew Scriptures, shared by both Jews and Christians, include condemnations of excessive wealth in the midst of increasing poverty.[59] Both Christian and Jewish scriptures include visions of a new creation at the end of history. This will be a time when enmity and hatred will cease and justice and peace will reign.[60] With these scriptures providing the ethical norms for political and economic life, religious lobbyists are driven to create a new vision for the United States. Because the values are far-reaching, the vision is broad. As a result, religious lobbyists often have an extensive agenda that is not confined to one "religious" issue area.

Because they are driven by religious values, religious lobbyists are often not concerned about earthly wins or losses. Faithfulness—not success—is their predominant goal. George Chauncey, the Washington lobbyist for the Presbyterian Church–U.S.A., captures this spirit when he says:

> Confidence in God's love and grace . . . should free us to take risks, to support hopeless causes, even to fail. Some people are compulsively careful in their politics. . . . Their main preoccupation is with what is "politically feasible." They would rather stay out of the fight than lose. . . . But surely, faithfulness to the cause of peace and justice rather

than the feasibility of political proposals ought to be the primary concern of believers.[61]

Biblical texts are thousands of years old, yet the prophetic challenge of government has waxed and waned. Why has the contemporary period seen a rise in this prophetic activism? By way of explanation, Robert Bellah contends that the traumatic events of the 1960s and 1970s challenged Americans' faith in their nation's higher purpose. Interestingly, different religious leaders and organizations have identified different traumatizing events. For religious conservatives, these were the Supreme Court decision in *Roe* v. *Wade*, the movement for an Equal Rights Amendment, and a growing perception that society is increasingly dominated by a secular liberal interest. For religious liberals, the traumas were the Vietnam War and the end of the Great Society. These different events symbolized a government with misplaced priorities.[62] In response, religious lobbyists increasingly heralded their prophetic critique.

Not all religious organizations rally around the prophetic political agenda of religious lobbyists. Indeed, many religious organizations do not sully themselves in the political process at all! Some simply ratify or legitimate existing structures and processes. But among religious lobbyists who enter the fray in Washington, the persistent pattern of political activity is radical criticism. While most secular lobbyists press for incremental change on a narrow range of issues, religious lobbyists shake the foundations of the entire political structure. When religious groups succeed, a major transformation of society usually takes place. Such transformations occurred as a result of the abolitionist movement, the prohibitionist movement, the civil rights movement, and the recent efforts of the Christian right. In each case, religious lobbyists responded to societal upheavals and injustices by challenging core values and posing alternatives. Troubled by and shocked at the priorities of government, religious lobbyists dug in their righteous heels, armed with their tradition of faith, and did battle with the principalities and powers. That effort continues to-day.

Religious lobbyists are motivated by a vision in which religious values dominate the state. At the same time, religious lobbyists affirm both religious liberty and the separation of church and state. Religious lobbyists do not support any type of theocracy or limitations on religious liberty. But they do support their right to vigorously petition the government to change its ways. Like other religious leaders who call for the veneration of the state, lobbyists seek to involve religion in politics. But for religious lobbyists, that connection is one of scathing criticism. While civil priests confer their shallow blessing, religious lobbyists sometimes seek to overturn the moneychangers' tables. Their criticism is not a polite one demurred over in a cozy dinner in a posh Washington restaurant. Rather, the indictment is so fundamental that religious lobbyists call for a large-scale reordering of government's very priorities. In a new way, they are describing their own version of the "city on a hill." Like the early Puritans who first used that metaphor, religious lobbyists seek a government that conducts itself with such high values that it can bear witness to all nations. By caring for the poor and remaining faithful to fundamental moral principles, the United States can be a shining beacon of hope for all nations.

3
CHAPTER

Theoretical Perspectives

THE INADEQUACY OF PLURALISM

Since James Madison, students of American politics have extolled the vices and virtues of groups. For Madison, the central reality of politics was groups, which he referred to as "factions." Madison feared that some groups could threaten democratic government. To defend against groups who sought to suppress liberty, Madison advocated a constitution that could cure the "mischiefs of faction." A large republic featuring "the separation of power" and "checks and balances" would make it difficult for pernicious factions to control government. Justice would prevail because the process of representative government would diminish the power of groups that threatened liberty.

In modern political science, pluralist theorists took up the Madisonian mantle and asserted that a focus on groups was the *sine qua non* of political analysis. In the twentieth century, Arthur Bentley,[1] David Truman,[2] and Robert Dahl contended that all aspects of politics could be understood as an outcome of group conflict. While other political analysts focused on the institutions of government (Congress, the presidency, the courts) and the motives and perceptions of the individual, pluralists called for a fixation on groups. Institutions and individuals were important, but the essence of politics was group conflict.

Pluralists see an array of interests or shared attitudes in society as the genesis of politics. These interests are transformed into organized interest groups because of "disturbances" that compel individuals to band together and begin what Truman calls the "inevitable gravitation to government."[3] Truman speaks of two kinds of disturbances that incite interests to organize. The first is the reaction to the increasing complexity of society. New developments such as computers or other technology may cause new groups to form. The second kind of disturbance is a cataclysmic event. Examples would be severe economic downturns, unfavorable legislation, or wars. These disturbances cause people to form groups to remedy the initial disturbance.[4]

Group formation can itself serve as a disturbance. Groups form in response to the appearance of other groups. The emergence of groups continues until an equilibrium is reached. Government then acts as a referee by formulating public policy in accordance with the varying amounts of pressure generated by groups. Public policy is a compromise among the different groups active on any given issue. The key to understanding politics is to focus on the activity of competing groups.[5]

While focusing on groups, pluralist theorists say little about the types of tactics used by organized interests to petition government. They merely say that groups will form and generate pressure on the state. The vagueness of their discussion of group pressure is a major weakness of pluralism. Furthermore, pluralism says little about the expectations of pressure groups concerning the resolution of their conflict. Organized religious interests work to exert pressure in the classic pluralist sense, but their expectations of fundamental political change lead them to reject a mainstream style of political compromise and incremental change. Religious lobbyists often believe that certain public policies are fundamentally wrong; an incremental or compromise solution to those policy errors is equally unacceptable. As a result of these political goals, religious lobbyists will choose different strategies. To explain this reality, a more nuanced theory of interest group politics is necessary.[6]

Theodore Lowi explained differences in political strategies using the concept of issue areas. Lowi argued that differing expectations lead to a differing style of politics. Because expectations are determined by the type of policy, different policy types will lead to different policy processes. Depending on whether one felt that the distribution of benefits was regulatory, distributive, or redistributive, different political strategies would result. Similarly, the political behavior of organized religious interests requires a different explanation because religious lobbyists expect and work for more far-reaching change than most lobbyists. Religious lobbyists seek fundamental, not incremental, change.[7]

TOWARD A NEW THEORY OF PROPHETIC LOBBYING

In its discussion of political strategies, pluralism is narrow. According to Lowi, "The pluralist model stresses conflict and conflict resolution through bargaining among groups and coalitions organized around shared interests."[8] Pluralist theory contends that lobbyists will use two types of tactics; neither is defined clearly. First is the attempt to maintain and expand one's coalition in order to maximize "pressure" on government. Second is the bargaining process among opposing coalitions and groups. In the bargaining process, the institutions of government work to manage the competition among opposing pressure groups by arranging compromises and balancing interests. According to Earl Latham,

> What may be called public policy is actually the
> equilibrium reached in the group struggle at any given

> moment, and it represents a balance which the contending
> factions or groups constantly strive to tip in their favor. . . .
> The legislature referees the group struggle.[9]

Most theorists reject this extreme view in which the state
is a mere scale that measures the relative pressure of
groups. Pluralists acknowledge that the state is not completely neutral; it has some autonomous power. Charles
Lindblom states that the policy process viewed in this way
is one of "partisan mutual adjustment." In this process,
"both state agencies and interest groups adjust their behavior to one another's intentions and power,"[10] The result is a
policy process in which all participants compromise and
the resulting change is incremental.[11] Both losers and win-
ners are usually willing to accept the compromise because
they believe that some change is better than no change. The
losers also may believe that their side may prevail in future
policy struggles.

Beyond the concepts of bargaining or compromise, the
tactics of this incremental pluralist process are not clearly
specified. Scholars have made no connection between an acceptance of incremental change and specific lobbying tactics. This is the looseness of pluralism. In studies of interest
group behavior,[12] authors merely list tactics with little
discussion of why lobbyists use the tactics that they do.
Hrebenar and Scott make a distinction between direct and
indirect lobbying.[13] (Other scholars use the terms "insider"
and "outsider" to define these two types of strategies.) Insider or "direct lobbying is defined as those tactics which
bring the official representatives of an organization or organizations into direct contact with governmental officials."
These include such familiar tactics as visiting legislators,
communicating information, testifying at a public hearing,
serving on advisory committees and boards, and of course
arranging the power lunch and other social contacts.[14] Outsider or "indirect lobbying . . . is more circuitous." Generally, it involves the generation of grassroots pressure
through letter-writing campaigns, protests, demonstrations,

and the use of the media.[15] Hrebenar and Scott describe both of these strategies in great detail. They tell which strategies are used, and they point out that indirect tactics are on the rise, but they do not work to develop a theory to tell us why a group will use a specific type of tactic. As a result, we are left without a coherent theoretical structure from which patterns of behavior can be explained.

The problem is made more complex with the presence of groups that seek more fundamental or radical—rather than incremental—change.[16] A refusal to accept a compromise will mean that policy is not a reflection of the balance of group and state agency pressures. Instead, the policy process becomes a winner-take-all situation in which the notions of bargaining and pressure have less relevance. For organized interests, this perspective will result in a change in behavior. In its present form, pluralist theory has trouble accommodating groups—like organized religious interests—that resist compromise. To explain the more radical politics of organized religious interests, revisions in pluralist theory are necessary.

There is only a small amount of literature that focuses on explaining radical politics. Such literature also works to distinguish radical from more mainstream politics. In a recent book, Lowi revised his well-known categorization of issue areas to take account of the "new" politics of public interest groups on the right or left. He pointed out that the politics of these groups is different because their politics is radical. Radical politics polarizes policy debates and makes compromise extremely difficult if not impossible (Figure 1). Lowi points out that the *Oxford English Dictionary* defines radical as "of or pertaining to a root or roots."

> It is associated with extremes precisely because people who insist on getting to the root of things are likely to express themselves intensely, rejecting the rules and procedures designed to produce compromise—in other words, rejecting mainstream or ordinary politics. . . . What is a rather fuzzy frontier for the mainstream is a formalized

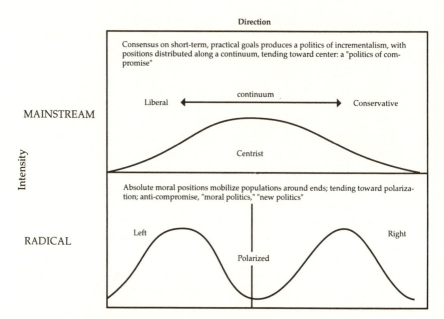

FIGURE 1   Public Philosophy: Mainstream and Radical

Source: Theodore J. Lowi, "Foreword: New Dimensions in Policy and Politics," in Raymond Tatalovich and Byron W. Daynes, *Social Regulatory Policy: Moral Controversies in American Politics,* 1988, p. xiii. Reprinted by permission of Westview Press, Boulder, CO.

border between radicals. . . . Positions are distributed accordingly . . . as a bimodal distribution. So consistently is radical politics polarized that this distribution has to be maintained in any diagrammatic analysis.[17]

The major political consequence of this moral perception of policy issues is the radicalization of the policy process. The "political behavior is more ideological, more moral, more directly derived from fundamental values, more intense, less utilitarian, more polarized, and less prone to compromise."[18] Because both liberal and conservative religious activists have goals of radical political change, we can expect a common form of political behavior. In Lowi's words, "In the world of morality and radicalization, the left and the right are a unity of opposites, together as one, logically and empirically apart from the mainstream."[19] The common political strategy of both liberals and conservatives is a radical style of politics that stresses the avoidance of compromise.

Religious activists are not the only activists who refuse to compromise. In the literature on party activists, some scholars have looked at the distinction between professionals and amateurs or purists. Stated simply, professionals have victory as their primary goal. Purists seek allegiance to a set of moral principles or policy positions—irrespective of the possibilities of attracting enough support to win. Aaron Wildavsky wrote about these categories of delegates in the 1964 Republican convention.[20] According to Wildavsky,

> The distinguishing characteristics of the purists [include] their emphasis on internal criteria for decision, on what they believe "deep down inside"; their rejection of compromise; their lack of orientation toward winning; their stress on the style and purity of decision—integrity, consistency, adherence to internal norms.[21]

The success of the purists in the 1964 convention led to the nomination of Goldwater and one of the biggest landslide losses in American history. Similarly, many argue that the purists in the Democratic party dominated the 1972 convention, which nominated another principled yet losing candidate, George McGovern. Jeane Kirkpatrick's analysis of delegates to the 1972 Democratic convention reveals the distinctive characteristics of the McGovern delegates.[22]

In contrast to the purists are the professionals. While professionals are not entirely unprincipled, they are more concerned with winning and losing. According to Wildavsky,

> The belief in compromise and bargaining; the sense that public policy is made in small steps rather than big leaps; the concern with conciliating the opposition and broadening public appeal; and the willingness to bend a

little to capture public support are all characteristics of the
traditional [or professional] politician in the United States.[23]

The purist disagreement with this statement is stark. In the
words of one Goldwater delegate, "I'd rather stick by the
real principles this country was built on than win. Popu-
larity isn't important; prestige isn't important; it's the principles that matter."[24]

Many religious activists have infiltrated political parties,
primarily the Republican party.[25] There they engage in the
same kind of purist behavior that the Goldwater delegates
used in 1964. In the lobbying community, religious activists
are driven by religious principles and act in a similar purist
manner. They are unwilling to compromise, and they adopt
a strategy that is different from that of other lobbyists.

Because of their unwillingness to compromise, religious
lobbyists favor an "outsider" strategy over an "insider"
strategy. If they were more willing to compromise, religious
lobbyists would engage in more insider tactics such as as-
sisting legislators in negotiating legislative language. But
they worry that this negotiation and bargaining could become a kind of bargain with the devil. Because they seek
more fundamental change, religious lobbyists look outward
to generate additional pressure for more vital change. They
seek to expand their coalition for fundamental reform. Occasionally, when their coalition is sufficient, they utilize insider tactics to negotiate their victory. But those moments
are rare. Most of their efforts are directed at articulating
their vision of a new America and inviting citizens to join
them. In Chapters 5 and 6, I will illustrate the tactics and
strategies of religious lobbyists more fully.

THEORIES OF OLIGARCHY: WHEN LEADERS
IGNORE MEMBER OPINION

Many have charged that prophetic religious lobbyists ignore the views of their members and lobby in oligarchical

fashion. Writing in 1915, Robert Michels argued that all group leaders tend to ignore their members. Michels termed this tendency an iron law of oligarchy. Groups are oligarchical because of both organizational necessity and the psychological processes in group leaders. Michels contended that groups seeking to reform and challenge existing power structures must themselves become oligarchical in order to challenge entrenched power successfully. Although group leaders initially state that this oligarchy is only a temporary requirement in a time of transition, Michels argued that the oligarchy becomes permanent because leaders, once they have successfully wielded power, come to believe in their own superiority and efficacy. Therefore, they work to retain the oligarchical power structure. The result is the creation of a power structure that is unresponsive to the needs of members.[26]

Some scholars have written that oligarchy is particularly inevitable in large organizations. Writing at about the same time as Michels, George Simmels contended that large groups demand and involve less of their members.[27] Mancur Olson[28] asserts that "the membership and power of large pressure-group organizations does not derive from their lobbying achievements, but is rather the by-product of their other activities." Olson strikingly argues that members do not always join groups for the larger political goal advocated by the group's lobbyists. He contends that individuals can enjoy that large collective good whether they join the group or not.

Instead, individuals join groups for other benefits that they receive only if they join and remain in a group. Olson calls these benefits selective incentives. For example, workers in a "closed shop" often join a union to get a job, not to support the union's lobbying efforts. Individuals may join an environmental group without thinking about environmental legislation, but primarily to receive a beautiful calendar.[29] In the extreme case, members are indifferent to the lobbying activities of leaders and care only about the provision of selective incentives. For example, many American Medical Association members join only to practice medicine; they do not care about the lobbying activities of their leaders. In similar situations, internal democracy becomes a moot point. As long as selective incentives are provided, members will remain indifferent to the political behavior of leaders. Lobbying then becomes a by-product.

When lobbying is a by-product, the link between member opinions and leader actions is severed. The result is an internal oligarchy that differs from the oligarchy of Michels but shares a lack of member participation in group decision making. In institutional religious interests, a similar situation sometimes prevails. Though religious leaders and lobbyists are intensely interested in politics, most members join churches and synagogues with no thought of the organization's political activity. The end result is a set of conditions that provide a perfect situation for "by-product" lobbying.[30]

RELIGIOUS JUSTIFICATIONS OF OLIGARCHICAL LOBBYING

Religious leaders justify nondemocratic decision making with theological reasons. They contend that the goal of religious organizations is to "discern God's will, not the members' interests." The obvious problem emerges when there are competing interpretations about the will of God. In response to such disagreements, a church or synagogue may resort to a democratic process to resolve disagreements. Alternatively, religious organizations may turn to church leaders whom they have ordained with additional authority. The interpretations of those leaders—rabbis, priests, pastors, popes, or elders—are given priority over political compromises and the views of lay members.

One powerful example in the Judeo-Christian tradition

is the leadership of Moses. Political scientist Aaron Wildavsky has written about Moses as a political leader. Part of his argument refers to the way in which Moses used his authority to try to transform the beliefs and behavior of the Israelites. Some authoritative behavior was seen as an essential dimension of religious leadership. The Ten Commandments came from God, not a majority vote. In churches and religious interest groups, many leaders could rationalize an oligarchical decision-making structure by arguing that it is necessary to preserve some representation of religious truth. If they were not oligarchical, then no one would speak out for the true faith. Democratic procedures are illegitimate if they lead to the advocacy of policies that are inconsistent with the religious principles of churches and synagogues.[31]

James R. Wood, a sociologist, integrates this theological justification into his analysis of religious organizations. He argues that leaders must transcend the organization and be faithful to religious values.

> Leaders do transcend member values. This is not
> illegitimate because leaders have a responsibility to
> respond to the core values of their church. They are not . . .
> using organizational resources for their own purposes.[32]

According to this view, religious organizations should not always be democratic. Following this logic, religious leaders often state that they must be faithful to God rather than the opinion polls of their members. Elliott Corbett, former chief Washington lobbyist for the United Methodist Church, spoke about this issue in the context of church involvement in the Vietnam issue. He stated that if the church waited until it had member backing,

> what, in the meantime, would have happened to the
> prophetic voice of the church? . . . Where deep moral
> issues are involved, the church cannot afford to wait for
> most of its members to agree before it exercises leadership.

> Church statements . . . should not be issued after the
> Gallup poll has made it clear they are safe; they should
> be proclaimed as a sort of "advance conscience" of the
> church.[33]

Elliot Corbett provides a clear example of religious lobbyists assuming the prophetic mantle. As always, it is unclear whether Corbett was a true prophet. He may have simply claimed a prophetic identity to gain power for the church agency in which he worked. Other individuals may be more prophetic than he. What is significant for this study is that he and other religious lobbyists see themselves as prophets. When they challenge the political and the religious establishments on issues such as war and peace, they claim that they are acting in accord with the radical demands of faith. Their interpretation of those demands—not member opinion—leads them to action.

THEORIES OF DEMOCRATIC DECISION MAKING: WHEN LEADERS RESPOND TO MEMBER OPINION

In actual practice, religious organizations reveal a mix of oligarchical and democratic decision making. The analytical challenge is to explain the changing relationship between leaders and members. Why does it vary from issue to issue? Why do leaders and members agree on some issues yet disagree on others? Why might prophetic religious lobbyists modify their views in the face of conflicting member opinion? Theories of democratic decision making may answer these questions.

Theologically, there are reasons to expect a more democratic process. A central principle of the Protestant Reformation was the primacy of the individual conscience over the church hierarchy. Often drawing support from the Protestant Reformation, many American churches were founded on the principles of the autonomy of individuals and congregations.[34] Many immigrants came to America in reaction to European state churches they found oppressive. As a result, there are theological and sociological reasons to expect alternatives to oligarchy in the internal politics of religious organizations.

Similarly, a number of scholars have attempted to develop empirical tests of Michels' iron law of oligarchy. The results show that oligarchy may not be inevitable in organizations. Lipset and his colleagues found that the International Typographical Union had a democratic internal process. A number of internal factions regularly competed for power, and occasionally there were major shifts in control of the union.[35] Other scholars have criticized Michels' work, arguing that he overstated the tendency to oligarchy.[36] In religious organizations, there is also a long history of popular protest of the actions of church leaders. As a result, oligarchy may not be the only organizational option for religious organizations.

Similarly, Mancur Olson's by-product lobbying may not be inevitable in all organizations. The driving logic of Olson's theory is the economically self-interested individual that is at the heart of economic theory. As such, Olson's theory has value only for a limited range of interest groups —that is, economic groups. Olson, himself, states,

> In philanthropic and religious lobbies the relationships between the purposes and interests of the individual member, and the purposes and interests of the organization, may be so rich and obscure that a theory of the sort developed here cannot provide much insight.[37]

As a strictly economic theory, Olson's work is limited in scope, and the by-product lobbying that he predicts may not be present in all organizations.

To explain this more complex picture, we need a theory that is applicable to noneconomic groups and capable of explaining both oligarchy and responsiveness to member opinion. A work that preserves the framework of rational individualism while extending its application to noneconomic groups is the exchange theory of Robert Salisbury and James Q. Wilson.[38] As in Olson's model, group formation is dependent on an exchange between leader and member. A member will agree to join a group in exchange for a particular benefit. But whereas economic groups focus primarily on material benefits, the transactions between leaders and members of noneconomic organizations are more complex. Leaders and members of noneconomic groups seek a broader range of goals.

To explain this broader range of goals, Salisbury and Wilson have extended Olson's exchange model. In addition to material benefits, leaders can offer solidary and purposive incentives. They can offer these incentives to group members in exchange for their participation and support. If they offer solidary and material benefits, it is possible for them to "purchase" member loyalty without member agreement with the lobbying goals and activity of leaders. But if members are interested in purposive incentives, then member participation in group decisions is necessary. Lobbying as a by-product is virtually impossible.

A refinement of the basic argument of exchange theorists is provided by Albert Hirschman.[39] Hirschman specifies the options that members have in their participation in organizational life. He claims that members have three options: exit, loyalty, and voice. First, members can express disapproval by exiting the organization, or "voting with their feet." Second, they can decide that their disagreements are not significant enough for them to contest. In this case they would remain loyal to an organization even though they disagree with some of the organization's actions. In addition to the first two options, members can make use of the participatory structures to voice their concerns and try to work for organizational change.

These developments in the exchange theory of internal

politics lead to a conclusion that nondemocratic internal politics is not inevitable. Organizations can assume a number of forms. Organizational leaders must choose from a number of organizational options, each of which bears a specific array of costs and benefits with it. The type of internal politics varies according to the goals and orientations of both leaders and members. Leaders may act either in congruence with or in opposition to member opinion. Members can respond with exit, voice, or loyalty.

TOWARD A REVISED EXCHANGE THEORY: EXPLAINING BOTH OLIGARCHICAL AND DEMOCRATIC DECISION MAKING

Though there are many theories that explain both democratic and nondemocratic internal group process, data to support these theories are scarce.[40] The evidence is thin because the existing literature provides only a beginning explanation of the nature of the relationship between leaders and members. There is little work that has specified when to expect changes in the form of internal politics. One reason for the shortcomings of this work is its exclusive focus on the relationship between leaders and members. It is clear that the interaction of leaders and members is the central dimension of internal politics, but it is also clear that interest groups are influenced by a variety of environmental forces. Similar actions by organization leaders can elicit completely different member responses depending on the context or environment. In one situation, members may remain loyal to an organization despite their disagreement with the positions and actions of leaders. In another situation, members may respond to the same action by exiting the organization.

This oscillation occurs because the environment can change the value of the differing resources that leaders and members possess. Any explanation of internal politics must take these environmental factors into account. John Mark Hansen begins to do so by stating that "people in different contexts have different preferences and resources and hence different subjective weightings of the benefits and costs of group participation."[41] Hansen argues that the context can affect people's willingness to take risks. Consequently, different contexts can alter the exchange value of selective benefits. In developing his "context-sensitive" model of group membership, Hansen looks at how changes in economic conditions affect membership decisions in three national organizations: the American Farm Bureau Federation, the League of Women Voters, and the National Association of Home Builders. Hansen finds that economic downturns cause individuals to join groups in exchange for collective benefits. To be sure, the individuals would enjoy the collective benefit regardless of their decision to join a group; nonetheless, many join the group. Hansen is arguing in effect that economic distress changes the price of collective or purposive benefits. In a context of economic hardship, the "prices" of these benefits will be cheaper. As a result, more people will be willing to pay the price and join the group.

Similarly, context alters the values of the benefits exchanged between leaders and members. As a result, different situations will necessitate or allow different types of decision making. In one context, democratic accountability is essential. In another situation, a nondemocratic or oligarchical process may be safely chosen by organizational leaders. The analytical challenge is to define context so that these two situations can be distinguished.

Richard Fenno's venerable work on congressional committees may be a useful beginning. He argues that the politics of congressional committees varies because of differences in the outsiders who take an interest in the policy concerns of each committee. Fenno conceptualizes the behavior of congressional committees by referring to both the goals of committee leaders and the role of outsiders: non-committee members of the House of Representatives or the Senate, the executive branch, clientele groups, and party leadership. For Fenno, the environment is the range of interested outsiders. Members of Congress must then reconcile their own goals with the interests of outsiders. The key question is to determine when a group leader will consent to the influences of various parts of the environment.[42] Building upon this work, David Price argues that one must think of the environment as "fields of incentives, opportunities, and constraints that shape their priorities and strategies." Changes in the nature of the environment change the way in which leaders determine how "profitable" a given course of action can be.[43]

Similarly, the behavior of interest group leaders will depend on both the views of their constituents and the interacting effect of the policy environment. This statement assumes that interest group leaders want both to continue to work for fundamental policy change and to maintain the viability of their organization. Achieving these goals requires an exchange of benefits between leaders and members that can lead to an "organizational surplus." Religious leaders can use the surplus to lobby on issues in which members disagree with their positions. The environment of most religious organizations will affect the nature of the exchange and the value of the surplus.

In religious organizations, many members did not join to achieve their political goals. Recent poll data support this claim. A Gallup poll showed that more than half of Americans think that churches should not persuade legislators. This group includes 54 percent of mainline Protestants and 53 percent of Catholics. Only among evangelical Protestants does a majority take the opposite position and support church lobbying.[44] As further evidence, another Gallup poll asked questions about why people were involved in churches. Lobbying was not even on the list.[45] The cumulative picture shows that, with the exception of evangelical Protestants, only a minority are interested in or supportive of lobbying by their leaders.

Because members are apathetic toward their church's lobbying, leaders have much latitude in their lobbying activity. But the freedom is not infinite; it is more like a limited surplus that leaders can use for lobbying. Sometimes, members may object to the lobbying effort of leaders and leave the organization or voice their concerns. In order to avoid this situation, religious lobbyists will practice a strategy of "blame avoidance."[46] If they have political goals that conflict with member opinion, they will pursue those goals only until members might become agitated enough to criticize the leadership.

The presence of this strategy represents a pragmatic departure from their purist pursuit of radical goals. In some ways this finding is ironic or unexpected; however, religious lobbyists realize that they must maintain their organization in order to provide a platform for their lobbying efforts. If their office becomes the target of harsh member criticism, their lobbying surplus will quickly disappear, and the very possibility of religious lobbying will be threatened. To a group of people who believe that political action is an essential part of faith, this outcome is worse than the pragmatic accommodation of the blame avoidance strategy. My theory predicts that religious lobbyists, in order to preserve their organization and—more importantly—their ability to lobby on a broad range of issues, will minimize their lobbying on a small subset of issues.

The salience of issues affects the relationships between leaders and members and the political strategies that leaders choose. My hypothesis is that religious leaders will reject a democratic form of internal politics only on low-salience issues. In Figure 2, this process is called safe oligarchy (quadrant IV). Members will allow their leaders to lobby in disagreement with their preferences only when

	High salience	Low salience
Leader-member agreement	I Democratic decision making	II Democratic decision making
Leader-member disagreement	III Risky oligarchy	IV Safe oligarchy

FIGURE 2   A Theory of Internal Politics

they are unconcerned or even indifferent about the consequences. In these situations, they will allow their leaders to use their surplus, and lobbying will be a by-product of the organization. On contentious high-salience issues, which are of concern to members, leaders will avoid offending member opinion because they know members are likely to protest. In Figure 2 this behavior is termed risky oligarchy and is found in the lower left-hand quadrant. Here, leaders are unable to afford the cost required to generate the necessary surplus for their prophetic political actions.

So, the relevant environment for religious lobbyists is the salience of issues. On low-salience issues, when members are not likely to be aware of the lobbying activities of their leaders, religious lobbyists are free to ignore member opinion (quadrant IV). On highly contentious issues where there is disagreement between leaders and members, no lobbying is likely to take place (III). This analysis, of course, also leaves the possibility for lobbying on issues of either high or low salience on which there is agreement between leaders and members (I and II). Undoubtedly these are the issues on which religious lobbyists are most influential. In Chapter 6 the picture developed here is painted in greater detail and the issues of religious lobbyists are explored.

4
CHAPTER

The Scope of the Prophetic Lobby

The membership of religious organizations is more diverse and extensive than that of other organizations. As mentioned previously, more than two-thirds of U.S. citizens claimed membership in a religious organization in 1988.[1] This proportion is greater than that of any other group.[2] In contrast, only 18–20 percent of the population belong to a labor union or other professional organization with collective bargaining capacity. Though there are no data on the number of people in business groups, the maximum membership is all those who work in business, approximately 16 percent of the population.[3] Clearly church and synagogue membership is the most inclusive organizational affiliation in the United States.

Religious lobbying, then, makes American politics more democratic by involving citizens in the political process who ordinarily might go unrepresented. Members of religious organizations range from the poor to the multimillionaire, the educated to the illiterate. They are spread all across the country. While many upper-class people are religious, no other organization includes as many poor and middle-class people in its ranks. Assessing membership data, James Q. Wilson stated that lower-income members dominate church membership to a greater degree than they

dominate any other major organization.[4] Thus the politicization of organized religion could serve as a significant
challenge to the well-documented tendency of upper- and
middle-class people to participate more in politics than
lower-class people.[5] Paul Weber states similarly that "iden-
tifiable religious societies are important for interest group
theory partially because they are by far the largest nonelite
group in the nation."[6] Clearly, organized religion has the
potential to make the universe of Washington lobbyists
more representative of the interests of nonelite citizens.

In the real world of politics, a large membership does not
always translate to a powerful lobbying presence in Washington. To assess the dimensions of the religious lobby ac-
curately, two factors were appraised: the number and the
size of organized religious interests. As a portion of the entire interest group universe of Washington, only 1 percent
of the approximately 7,000 organized interests in Washington are religious groups (Table 1). Counting numbers of organizations, it is clear that the religious lobby is only a
small fraction of the interest group community. The vast
majority of lobbyists, approximately 99 percent, are officially nonreligious.

But a simple count of groups may represent the extent of
influence inaccurately. Staff sizes and budgets can provide
a fuller picture. Using these measures, religious lobbyists
still remain a small fraction of all lobbyists in Washington
(see Table 2). Religious lobbyists reported that their organizations had a grand total of 273 persons on their staffs and
an aggregate budget total of over $27 million. Because some
lobbyists were unwilling to reveal the size of their budgets
and staffs, those numbers underestimate actual size. However, even if the estimates were doubled, it would be clear
that the physical presence of religious lobbyists is small.

Looking at individual organizations, religious lobbies
also appear small. Only five organizations had budgets of
$2 million or greater. None reported a staff larger than

TABLE 1
The Washington Interest Group Universe

CATEGORY	PERCENT OF TOTAL NUMBER OF ORGANIZATIONS
Religious organizations	0.7
Corporations	45.7
Trade and other business associations	24.4
Professional associations	6.9
Unions	1.7
Citizens' groups	3.4
Civil rights/social welfare/poor	1.9
Women/elderly/handicapped	1.1
Governmental units–U.S.	4.2
Other foreign	2.0
Other unknown	8.2

Source: Comparative data from *Organized Interests and American Democracy* by Kay Lehman Schlozman and John T. Tierney. Copyright © 1986 by Kay Lehman Schlozman and John T. Tierney. Reprinted by permission of HarperCollins Publishers, Inc.

thirty. Most organizations had staffs of ten or less and budgets under $500,000. For example, the Washington office of the Evangelical Lutheran Church in America, a church with 5 million members, has a staff of seven lobbyists and a budget of $300,000. The Washington office of the Methodist Church has a staff of eighteen and a budget of $2 million. The staff is charged with representing a church with 14 million members. Thus, there is approximately one staff person for every 800,000 members.

No comprehensive comparable data are available for the total numbers of staff and budgets of all the Washington lobbyists. However, some lone organizations rival the size of the entire religious community. For example, the govern-

TABLE 2
Staff Size and Budgets of Religious Interest Groups (1988)

LOBBYING ORGANIZATION	STAFF SIZE	BUDGET ($1,000)
U.S. Catholic Conference	15	n.a.
NETWORK	10	500
Catholic Charities	2	131
National Council of Churches	8	n.a.
Washington Office of the Episcopal Church	4	100
Presbyterian Church USA—Washington Office	10	n.a.
United Methodist Church, General Board of Church and Society	18	2,000
Evangelical Lutheran Church in America, Office of Governmental Affairs	7	300
United Church of Christ, Office for Church and Society	16	800
American Baptist Churches USA	4	200
American Friends Service Committee	3	150
Friends Committee on National Legislation	15	850
Mennonite Central Committee	4	120
Church of the Brethren, Washington Office	3	200
Baptist Joint Committee for Public Affairs	8	700
National Association of Evangelicals	7	n.a.
General Conference of Seventh Day Adventists	6	n.a.
Lutheran Church–Missouri Synod	2	114
Christian Voice	22	n.a.

TABLE 2 *Continued*

LOBBYING ORGANIZATION	STAFF SIZE	BUDGET ($1,000)
Concerned Women for America	25	10,000*
Family Research Council	14	3,000*
Christian Coalition	—	4,300*
American Jewish Committee	7	n.a.
American Jewish Congress	n.a.	n.a.
Union of American Hebrew Congregations	n.a.	n.a.
IMPACT	9	425
Religious Task Force on Central America	2	n.a.
Interfaith Action for Economic Justice	10	400
Association for Public Justice	2	150
Bread for the World	30	2,100
Christic Institute	7	2,200
Unitarian Universalist	3	83
Total	273	27,440

*Data derived from Roy Beck, "Washington's Profamily Activists," *Christianity Today* 36 (November 9, 1992): 21. All other data from member survey.

ment of Japan spent $60 million dollars to lobby Washington in 1992.[7] The National Alliance of Business had a budget of $12.5 million in 1981.[8] Other organizations dwarf the religious lobbies.

However, the numbers of lobbyists, budget amounts, and numbers of staff are imperfect indicators of an organization's presence and influence. Influence and power arise from a variety of factors. Because religious organizations represent, at least in the abstract, two-thirds of the U.S. public, religious lobbyists may have influence beyond the size of their budgets and staff. In addition to sheer numbers of members, religious organizations have unique claims to make. Primarily, they represent a tradition of belief to which members are powerfully attached. This tradition of belief has a history of thousands of years. Few other organizations can match the depth and fervency of religious belief. Finally, much religious rhetoric contains proclamations of the weak triumphing over the strong. In the Old Testament, David slays the giant Goliath. In the New Testament Gospel of Luke, Mary the mother of Jesus speaks of a God who "scattered the proud . . . put down the mighty from their thrones . . . filled the hungry with good things, and the rich he has sent empty away."[9] In the biblical tradition, possessing less worldly power is not necessarily viewed as a shortcoming. Indeed, weakness is sometimes understood as a strength. With commitment so deep, it is possible for underfinanced groups to be inspired to triumph.

Aside from such rhetoric and the claim to represent two-thirds of America, religious lobbyists have a small presence in Washington. Part of the reason for this is that citizens do not join religious organizations to advance their public policy goals. In fact, many members of religious organizations *object deeply* to any political involvement by their church or synagogue. Most join the organization for other reasons: to deepen their personal faith, to meet friends, or to provide educational opportunities for their children. Because members usually have only a mild interest in politics, churches and synagogues devote only a small fraction of their resources to lobbying. Despite this ambivalence, the sheer size of many denominations and organizations is impressive and gives religious lobbyists significant latent strength. Government officials and other lobbyists may defer to religious lobbyists because of this potential power. If religious organizations are more fully involved in the political process, they can exert tremendous force.

THEOLOGICAL DIVERSITY

Several decades ago, it was easier to map the terrain of American religious life. As recently as the 1950s, Will Herberg wrote that American religious life could be summed up in a tripartite division of Protestants, Catholics, and Jews.[10] Much research has used this paradigm to structure its inquiry. More recently, the distinctions among religious communities have multiplied. Political scientist Ken Wald argues that recent trends "render hopelessly inadequate the traditional portrait of American religious identity encapsulated in [the] trinity of Protestant, Catholic, Jew."[11] Herberg's three categories have been divided into finer classifications. Jews have been split into Orthodox, Conservative, and Reformed; Catholics have tended to remain in one broad category; and the Protestant category has fractured into many different subgroups.

Denominations are the most common category of religious orientation. Yet, this classification has been complicated by the weakening attachment of individuals to their denomination. Many people change denominations several times in their lifetime.[12] With this new complexity, Ken Wald argues that new distinctions within denominations are now appropriate.[13] Yet lobbyists represent the entire denomination, not each faction. As a result, distinctions by denominational label are important for studying lobbying.

Protestant denominations are usually reduced to several categories. Mainline denominations are the Methodists, Presbyterians, Episcopalians, United Church of Christ, Lutherans, and American Baptists. These denominations are characterized by their acceptance of modern methods of biblical studies in which texts are not interpreted literally, but rather in their historical context. Evangelical and fundamentalist Protestants are in another category. Groups in these categories usually reject much modern Biblical scholarship and accept a more literalistic method of reading Scripture.

They are also more assertive about gaining new converts. Often, they feature an adult "born-again" experience as the criterion of individual membership. To these categories, some observers add a category of African-American Protestants. Most African-American Protestants have evangelical beliefs, but racial differences distinguish them from white evangelicals. Finally, "peace" Protestants are another category. The Mennonites, the Quakers, and the Church of the Brethren emphasize a commitment to pacifism as a central part of their beliefs.[14]

Evangelicalism is often equated with fundamentalism, but there are differences between the two. Reichley and Hertzke see fundamentalists as a subset of evangelicals.

> Evangelicalism is best defined as a branch of Christianity, descended from the pietist movement of the Reformation by way of the Great Awakening, that emphasizes the direct experience by the individual of the Holy Spirit (being "born again") and that regards the Bible as an infallible source of religious and moral authority. Fundamentalism is an extreme form of evangelicalism. All fundamentalists are evangelicals, but not all evangelicals are fundamentalists.[15]

This definition is consistent with a quote, attributed to Jerry Falwell, that a fundamentalist is "an evangelical who is upset." Some research disputes that fundamentalism is a subset of evangelicalism. Clyde Wilcox surveyed religious activists in Ohio and discovered that some fundamentalists did not want to refer to themselves as evangelicals. However, most observers see much overlap between the two categories. In this study, evangelicals and fundamentalists are put in separate categories. Table 3 shows the broader theological categories of organized religious interests.

The category of evangelical seems especially vague. When lobbyists were asked whether they considered their organizations evangelical, a number of groups not usually in that category responded affirmatively. Those groups not

TABLE 3
Theological Categories

Fundamentalist
  Moral Majority
  Christian Voice
  Concerned Women for America
Evangelical
  National Association of Evangelicals
  Lutheran Church–Missouri Synod
  General Conference of Seventh Day Adventists
  Family Research Council
Catholic
  NETWORK
  Catholic Charities
  U.S. Catholic Conference
  Christic Institute
Jewish
  American Jewish Committee
  American Jewish Congress
  Union of American Hebrew Congregations
Mainline Protestants
  Episcopal Church, Washington Office
  Evangelical Lutheran Church in America, Office for
    Governmental Affairs
  American Baptist Churches USA
  United Methodist Church, General Board of Church and
    Society
  United Church of Christ, Office for Church and
    Society
  Baptist Joint Committee for Public Affairs
  Presbyterian Church, USA
  Church Women United
Peace Protestant
  Mennonite Central Committee
  American Friends Service Committee
  Church of the Brethren, Washington Office
  Friends Committee on National Legislation

(continued)

TABLE 3 *Continued*

Broader coalitions
  IMPACT
  Religious Task Force on Central America
  Interfaith Action for Economic Justice
Other
  Association for Public Justice
  Bread for the World
  Unitarian Universalist

---

usually categorized as evangelicals are listed in Table 4. This finding contrasts with much contemporary scholarship that points to a more narrowly circumscribed evangelical universe. This discrepancy also points the vagueness and contestability of the term "evangelical." Kenneth Wald argued that people who call themselves evangelical vary greatly.[16] This should not be surprising when the root meaning of the word *evangelical* is unearthed. It is derived from a Greek word meaning the "proclamation of the good news."[17] While adherents to differing religious traditions disagree over the content of their theology, believers of most traditions want to share their particular version of the good news with others; therefore, they are evangelicals. Their theological content and approach may be different, but they claim an evangelical identity. For many, avoiding the evangelical label would be like a business leader proclaiming to be unconcerned with making a profit. Despite this broader usage of this term, most analysts classify evangelicals as described earlier.

However, the fact that many disparate lobbyists call themselves evangelical may point to underlying unity among groups not always considered allies. Perhaps these divergent groups could work together on some issues. Family values is a shared concern. Usually a province of the evangelical and fundamentalist right, it could become a

TABLE 4
Nontraditional Evangelicals

Evangelical Lutheran Church in America, Office for
  Governmental Affairs
Episcopal Church, Washington Office
American Baptist Churches USA
United Methodist Church, Board of Church and Society
United Church of Christ, Office for Church and Society
Baptist Joint Committee for Public Affairs
Mennonite Central Committee
U.S. Catholic Conference

unifying issue for the evangelical right and left. By joining together and forging common strategies, much political power can be attained. Such research is beyond the scope of this book, so I move now to the more central categories of this project, the political classification of organized religious interests.

POLITICAL CLASSIFICATION

When they cover religion in the 1980s and '90s, the media and academia usually focus on the activity of fundamentalist evangelical Protestants. This is a pronounced shift from earlier decades, particularly the 1960s. In that decade, liberal churches were at the forefront of the struggle to gain civil rights and end the Vietnam war. The media covered this activity, but gave scarcely a glance to the nascent religious right. In the 1990s, liberal religious activists are largely ignored, in part because of the decline of their influence. They do not seem to be at the vanguard of many political movements. Moreover, the secular liberal establishment has seemed to "banish religion" from their politics.

In contrast, secular conservatives have shrewdly formed

alliances with religious conservatives. The quadrennial conventions of the Republican and Democratic parties illustrate this contrast. While religious conservative groups conspicuously work to make the Republican party more conservative, liberal religious groups are invisible at Democratic conventions. Liberal religious activists are marginalized in ways their conservative colleagues are not.

To develop the full picture of the political beliefs of religious lobbyists, I asked group leaders to self-identify themselves as liberals, conservatives, or moderates on both economic and social issues (see Tables 5 and 6). In response, only 12 percent of lobbyists refused to self-identify; 50 percent of lobbyists identified their organizations as social and economic liberals; 17 percent called themselves social and economic conservatives; 17 percent called their organizations liberal on at least one dimension; and 4 percent called their organizations conservative on one dimension.

These findings are important responses for several reasons. First, one might expect religious lobbyists to resist putting ideological labels on their organizations. Such labeling could give the impression that an organization was a political movement in religious disguise. Despite this obstacle, only three lobbyists refused to self-identify. Second, it would not be surprising to find some resistance to the word *liberal*. In the campaign of 1988, politicians like George Bush successfully used the term as a derogatory epithet. In 1992, Bill Clinton triumphed in part by moving to the center and avoiding the liberal label. Despite the unpopularity of the label, approximately half of religious lobbyists called themselves liberal.

Self-identification may distort actual beliefs because people define liberal and conservative differently. To provide additional perspective on the political identity of the religious community, organizations were classified by their positions on five issues: (1) government spending to help the

TABLE 5
Self-Identification on Economic and Social Issues

Social and economic liberals (12)
   NETWORK
   Catholic Charities
   American Jewish Committee
   American Jewish Congress
   American Baptist Churches USA (liberal to moderate)
   Episcopal Church, Washington Office
   United Methodist Church, Board for Church and Society
   Church Women United
   IMPACT (liberal to moderate)
   National Council of Churches (liberal to moderate)
   American Friends Service Committee
   Church of the Brethren, Washington Office
Social liberals–economic moderates (3)
   Evangelical Lutheran Church in America, Office for Church in
     Society
   Mennonite Central Committee
   Unitarian Universalist
Social moderates–economic liberals (1)
   Interfaith Action for Economic Justice
Social moderates–economic moderates (2)
   General Conference of Seventh Day Adventists
   Association for Public Justice
   Social conservatives–economic conservatives (5)
   National Association of Evangelicals
Christian Voice
Family Research Council
Moral Majority
Concerned Women for America
Refused to self-identify (5)
   United Church of Christ
   Friends Committee on National Legislation
   Lutheran Church–Missouri Synod
   Baptist Joint Committee
   United States Catholic Conference

TABLE 6
Frequency Distribution of Economic and Social Positions

| | ECONOMIC ISSUES | | |
SOCIAL ISSUES	Conservative	Moderate	Liberal
Conservative*	5	0	0
Moderate	0	2	1
Liberal	0	3	12

*It may be significant that the five organizations at the conservative end of the table all identified themselves as fundamentalist or conservative evangelical. Two of the groups in the moderate-moderate category, the Seventh Day Adventists and the Lutheran Church–Missouri Synod, also were in the theologically conservative category. There seems to be a connection between theological and political beliefs. This is another topic for further research.

poor; (2) defense spending; (3) aid to the Nicaraguan Contras; (4) a constitutional amendment to ban abortion; and (5) school prayer. Following popular contemporary identification, a liberal position is one that supports increased government spending to help the poor, decreased defense spending, and cuts in military aid to the Nicaraguan contras and opposes a constitutional amendment to ban abortion and any legislation promoting organized school prayer. A conservative takes the opposite positions. In Table 7 a group is classified as liberal or conservative if it agrees with the liberal or conservative position on four out of five issues. A moderate group is one that agrees with the liberal or conservative position on two or three out of five positions.

Again, as shown in Table 7, the predominance of liberal religious lobbyists is revealed in the data. Eighteen groups are liberal, two groups are moderate, and three groups are conservative. Among the remaining groups not active on all

TABLE 7
Political Distinctions Based on Issue Positions

Liberal (18)
    U.S. Catholic Conference
    NETWORK
    National Council of Churches
    Washington Office of the Episcopal Church
    Presbyterian Church USA
    United Methodist Church, General Board of Church and
        Society
    Evangelical Lutheran Church in America, Office for
        Governmental Affairs
    United Church of Christ, Office for Church and Society
    American Baptist Churches USA
    Friends Committee on National Legislation
    Mennonite Central Committee
    Church of the Brethren, Washington Office
    American Jewish Committee
    American Jewish Congress
    Union of American Hebrew Congregations
    IMPACT
    Unitarian Universalist
    Church Women United
Moderate (2)
    National Association of Evangelicals
    Lutheran Church–Missouri Synod
Conservative (3)
    Christian Voice
    Concerned Women for America
    Moral Majority
Limited issue groups (9)
    Catholic Charities (tends liberal)
    American Friends Service Committee (tends liberal)
    Baptist Joint Committee (tends moderate)
    Religious Task Force on Central America (tends liberal)
    Interfaith Action for Economic Justice (tends liberal)
    Bread for the World (tends liberal)
    Christic Institute (tends liberal)
    Family Research Council (tends conservative)
    General Conference of Seventh Day Adventists (tends
        moderate)

five issues, six additional groups take liberal positions on the issues in which they are active. Two groups tend toward a moderate position and one group is closer to a conservative position. Again, this preponderance of liberal groups clashes with media interpretations that focus more attention on the conservative groups.

Conservative groups may get more attention because they possess more resources. Although their organizations are fewer in number, their budgets and staff are larger. Table 8 reveals these data. Because of missing data, it is difficult to draw a more complete conclusion. Nonetheless, liberal religious lobbying groups are an underreported part of religion and politics. Even when compared to conservative groups, they are a sizable presence in Washington.

However, the influence of conservatives should not be underestimated. Though religious conservatives may not make up a "moral majority," they have played a crucial role in U.S. national politics in recent years. The efforts of people like Jerry Falwell and Pat Robertson did much to get Ronald Reagan and George Bush elected. Continuing political pressure by religious lobbyists transformed the political agenda of the 1980s. Issues like school prayer and abortion could no longer be ignored.[19] In 1992, Bush had the most steadfast support from white and evangelical voters. Or-

TABLE 8
Total Staff and Budgets

	TOTAL STAFF	TOTAL BUDGET ($1,000)
Liberal groups	189	10,642
Moderate groups	23	814
Conservative groups	61	17,300

ganizations such as Pat Robertson's Christian Coalition worked for Bush, even though they would have preferred a more conservative candidate. In exchange, these groups gained a Republican platform that was very consistent with their beliefs, and they forced Bush to compromise and move to the right. In 1994, the religious right played a crucial role in the big gains of the Republican party. In many states, the religious right dominated the GOP and, across the country, energized Christian conservatives provided the margin of victory for many Republicans.[20]

Religious conservatives have withdrawn somewhat from Washington politics in the 1990s, but they continue to be very active at the state and local level. The Christian Coalition is not located in Washington, but it is located fairly close by in Chesapeake, Virginia. Though they expend much effort on state and local issues, they do lobby Washington from afar. They claim success in opposing Clinton's proposal to end the ban on gays in the military and the effort to use Medicaid funds to pay for abortions.[21] In elections of the 1990s, they distributed millions of voter guides that identified congressional votes on issues of importance and vigorously attacked President Clinton's agenda.[22]

In contrast, religious liberals have wielded less political clout, partly because they are ignored by a secular media. More importantly, they do not seem vitally connected with their constituency. For example, the Washington office of the Evangelical Lutheran Church in America, a mainline denomination of 5 million members, sends its *Legislative Update* to only 5,000 members. Although the office can reach other members through the media or through coalitions in which they are members, the newsletter subscribers are the portion of the church's membership that can be most easily mobilized. The predicament of the Lutheran Church is repeated in other mainline Protestant bodies. Most members of denominations are unaware that they have a lobbying office in Washington. As a result, denominational lobbying offices, most of which are liberal, are in danger of functioning as diminutive appendages of larger denominations. They do not have the active multimillion member constituency that the Christian right has.

Undoubtedly, members of Congress dismiss lobbies that do not have a vital connection to their members. Possessing neither the potential votes of members nor the campaign contributions of more well-heeled groups, some liberal groups are more easily marginalized than conservatives. To gain greater influence, they must either gain the support of their members or speak with such clarion moral force to persuade those who occupy the seats of power. Sometimes, this happens.

STRUCTURE OF ORGANIZED RELIGIOUS INTERESTS

For the most part, scholars of interest groups have ignored the diversity of the structure of interest groups and institutions. Robert Salisbury's article "Interest Representation: The Dominance of Institutions" is one exception. He argues that there are important distinctions between "institution, institutional interests and their advocacy, on the one hand, and what we have rather awkwardly called membership interest groups on the other."[23] This distinction requires substantial revisions in both theoretical and descriptive formulations of the governmental process. "A corporation, a local government, most churches, and even universities are different, not totally but in crucial ways, from our conventional notion of interest groups, and the traditional literature on the nature of interest groups does not tell us about the difference."[24]

In the universe of religious interest groups and institutions, there are a variety of structural forms. Many groups are traditional membership groups. But many others represent denominations, coalitions, or other institutional religious interests (see Table 9). The three major categories are

TABLE 9
The Structure of Organized Religious Interests

Membership groups (10)
  NETWORK
  Christian Voice
  Concerned Women of America
  Family Research Council
  Moral Majority
  American Jewish Congress
  American Jewish Committee
  Association for Public Justice
  Bread for the World
  Church Women United
Denominations (10)
  U.S. Catholic Conference
  Washington Office of the Episcopal Church
  Presbyterian Church USA
  United Methodist Church, General Board of Church and
    Society
  American Baptist Churches USA
  Friends Committee on National Legislation
  Church of the Brethren, Washington Office
  General Conference of Evangelicals
  Lutheran Church–Missouri Synod
  Union of American Hebrew Congregations
  Unitarian Universalist
Representatives of religious institutions (3)
  Catholic Charities
  American Friends Service Committee
  Mennonite Central Committee
Coalitions of denominations (6)
  National Council of Churches
  Baptist Joint Committee for Public Affairs
  National Association of Evangelicals
  IMPACT
  Interfaith Action for Economic Justice
  Religious Task Force on Central America
Other (1)
  Christic Institute

the traditional membership groups, the Washington representatives of large denominational bodies, and the coalitions of denominations. Salisbury argues that the growing proliferation of institutional representation requires the analytical attention of political scientists. Specifically, the claim to represent an institution might require a different form of political behavior than the claim to represent a membership group. However, most political scientists have not considered the possibility of such distinctive political behavior.

At issue is the claim to represent. According to Salisbury, member interests are not crucial in institutional representation; rather, the judgments of leaders concerning the requirements of institutional survival and growth are most crucial.[25] The separation between institutional and member interests is the central distinction between an institution and a membership group. Salisbury points to a university in which the "members," or students, are only transitory residents. As a result, trustees are admonished to balance both the future and the present needs of the institution. Similarly, corporate directors can be held liable if they do not exhibit some concern for long-term growth.[26]

Denominational church bodies are a distinctive form of institution because of the religious interest they must represent. Like nonreligious institutions, they must be concerned with the survival of the institution. Religious representatives are concerned with issues like establishing tuition tax credits for religious schools and maintaining the income-tax deduction for charitable gifts. But unlike their secular counterparts, representatives of religious institutions must be faithful to the religious tradition they are called to represent. Sometimes this requirement causes leaders to do things with which members may disagree.

To ensure both institutional survival and theological integrity, religious institutions have developed differing internal processes. Some church bodies, like the United States

Catholic Church, have few trappings of an internal democratic process. Other religious institutions, most notably Protestants, make decisions through a more democratic process. A major part of this process takes place at annual conventions that include grassroots representatives from every area of the country.[27] The position of the church on public policy issues is determined at these conventions. All the delegates are to vote in accordance to the demands of Scripture, not the expediency of institutional interests. Ironically, while the democratic mold is prevalent among Protestant organizations, there are frequent charges that lobbying by Protestant representatives is not representative of member opinion. This dilemma is more fully explored in Chapter 7.

5
CHAPTER

The Prophetic Outlook of Religious Lobbyists

In his study of Old Testament prophets, Abraham Heschel, a biblical scholar and Jewish rabbi, wrote, "Prophecy is the voice that God has lent to the silent agony, a voice to the plundered poor, to the profaned riches of the world."[1] Another biblical scholar, Walter Brueggemann, contended that "the task of prophetic ministry is to nurture, nourish, and evoke a consciousness and perception alternative to the consciousness and perception of the dominant culture around us."[2] To do that, biblical prophets express trenchant criticisms of the dominant social reality. Prophetic orations usually begin with a raging critique of the status quo, but they end with a vision of a transformed society. For Brueggemann, Moses is the archetypical prophet who rages against the imperial reality. In place of the pharaoh's social world, Moses proclaimed the alternative reign of God. He sought to dismantle the politics of oppression and counter it with a politics of justice and compassion.[3]

There are profound differences between religious lobbyists and the long tradition of prophets. Because they try to persuade Congress, religious lobbyists confine themselves to articulating a legislative agenda. Biblical prophets articulated a far more penetrating and comprehensive critique of entire societies. They criticized religious and political institutions as well as the ethics of all of society. Citizens, politicians, and religious leaders drew equal reproach. More than politics was at stake. Brueggemann contends that prophets went beyond specific public crises and instead addressed the ongoing domestication of prophetic vision. Sometimes public issues were involved, but there was something more enduring about the prophetic critique.[4] As a result, the words of biblical prophets were more disturbing and penetrating than anything emanating from modern-day religious lobbyists.

Yet there is something prophetic about religious lobbyists. To be sure, religious lobbyists may improperly claim the prophetic identity. That is, the claim to root a political vision in a religious tradition may be a disingenuous attempt to manipulate religion to gain political power. Allen Hertzke has called some religious lobbyists "cheap prophets."[5] It is surely beyond the scope of this book to assess the truth or falsity of religious lobbyists' prophetic vision, but they do understand their work and proclaim their vision in a prophetic way. Understanding religious lobbyists as prophets—whether true or false—can illuminate our understanding of their political endeavors.

Like biblical prophets, religious lobbyists criticize in a more strident manner than other social critics; sometimes they seem exaggerated. Many have derided religious lobbyists for this tendency. Yet their sometimes harsh voices resemble Heschel's description of biblical prophets. Heschel writes, "We and the prophet have no language in common. To us the moral state of society, for all its stains and spots, seems fair and trim; to the prophet it is dreadful."[6] In a prophetic way, religious lobbyists express deep disillusionment with the predominant values and trends of Washington politics. In religious terms, they see Washington as corrupt, and they fight for a vision of a new city, a new kingdom. They charge that contemporary problems are caused by the absence of religious values. They work to herald an alternate vision.

PROPHETIC DISILLUSIONMENT WITH WASHINGTON POLITICS

In contemporary politics, Christian conservatives articulate their disillusionment with Washington politics most clearly. Previously they ignored politics and wanted nothing to do with it. However, in the 1980s and '90s, they entered the political process in great numbers because of a negative reaction to their perceptions of secular, cosmopolitan, and liberal trends in America.[7] Several events seem critical. The Supreme Court rulings against school prayer (*Engel* v. *Vitale*, 1962) and in favor of legal abortion (*Roe* v. *Wade*, 1973) seemed particularly ominous. These rulings, as well as the growing power of the women's movement, the gay rights movement, and the peace movement, signaled growing iniquity in Washington. Increasingly, conservatives felt that government was attacking fundamental religious values. Gary Bauer of the Family Research Council recently contended that these changes will undermine the nation and end American life as we know it.[8] To save the nation, a lobbyist for the Moral Majority insisted that Christian lobbying was necessary.

> In the early 1980s, the political community was being projected as an uncivilized territory that only Christian thought could save. If we did not bring the ideas of biblical solutions, the country [would go] bankrupt.[9]

The leader of the Moral Majority, Jerry Falwell, wrote a book, *Listen America*, that presented the vision of Christian fundamentalists. The book contains separate chapters on the threats posed by secular humanists, feminists, and homosexuals.[10] According to Falwell, each of these groups violates religious values and threatens nothing less than the strength of America. In 1989, Falwell terminated his Washington organization and withdrew from active participation in Washington politics; however, his current television show still includes active references to the social issues that animated his work in Washington. His concerns are the same; he has only rejected Washington as the most promising place to address his concerns.[11]

Though it has reduced its Washington presence, Christian Voice is still present in the nation's capital. Its concerns echo those of Falwell and Bauer. In a pamphlet published in 1989, the organization declared its indictment of Washington politics and its call to action.

> Unless we, God's faithful, stand up and are counted, we could see our nation destroyed from moral decay and our precious liberties lost. Even worse, we will lose America as God's launching pad to preach Christ unto "all nations." We believe that the standards of Biblical morality (long the protection and strength of the nation), the sanctity of our families, the innocence of our young, and the very fiber of the Republic are crumbling under the onslaught of the powerful attack launched by the "rulers of darkness of this world" and insidiously sustained under the ever more liberal ethic.[12]

Disagreeing profoundly over the causes and remedies of America's problems, liberal lobbyists nonetheless express their criticism of the Washington establishment in a similar manner. Both conservatives and liberals see Washington as an immoral place, a place with misguided priorities and values. Both challenge the values and direction of government policy. Both see exploitation and oppression as the dominant social reality of Washington. A lobbyist for the U.S. Catholic Conference contrasted the Catholic tradition with the dominant thinking of Washington.

> In Catholic social teaching the fundamental starting point is the human person, the life, dignity and rights of the person. That is not the starting point for the Washington establishment.[13]

Paralleling the Catholic focus on human rights and dignity, other religious lobbyists also spoke of their advocacy of voices and values not heard in Washington. The lobbyist for IMPACT, a liberal ecumenical organization, said, "I think the religious community sees itself as here to speak for those whose voices will not be heard as the debates shift."[14] For liberal lobbyists, the silent voices are the cries of the poor. To them, ignoring the needs of the poor is the paramount failing of Washington politics. A lobbyist for the United Church of Christ contrasted his work with the work of most Washington lobbyists in this way:

> When I introduce myself informally, I sometimes call myself a poor people's advocate. I say that because I think the constituency that I am trying to give voice to and work with is the poor. In Washington, they don't have many advocates.[15]

Liberal religious lobbyists repeatedly affirmed their identity as advocates for the poor. Bob Tiller of the American Baptists said, "People who are defenseless, that's what we are here for. We are here to counter some of the other trends and groups, the thousands of lobbyists in this city who seem to represent the wealthy."[16] Similarly, a brochure from NETWORK claimed, "At last, the powers-that-be are paying attention! . . . For over 20 years we have lobbied for public policy on behalf of the poor and powerless in our nation and throughout the world."[17] Some lobbyists spoke of the small number of lobbyists in Washington who profess this position. Sally Timmel of Church Women United claimed that "for every twenty lobbyists representing the nonprivileged in Washington, there are twenty thousand

representing the privileged." She further contrasted the
fifty religious lobbyists working for peace with the three
thousand paid lobbyists for the Pentagon alone.[18] Before his
retirement, Ed Snyder of the Friends Committee for National Legislation was considered an unofficial dean of religious lobbyists because of his long tenure in Washington.

> Money talks and Congress listens. We try to represent the
> poor, the disadvantaged, both here and in other countries.
> They're vastly underrepresented, whereas people with
> money hire the high-priced lawyers. They make all the
> contacts on the hill and are way ahead.[19]

Like representatives of the liberal Protestant and Catholic
tradition, lobbyists for the Jewish tradition also spoke of the
chasm between their concern for the poor and the concerns
of most of Washington. Their work is rooted in a tradition
of Jewish concern for social justice. Glen Stein of the Union
of American Hebrew Congregations said,

> We like to think we represent the people of whom
> Roosevelt was thinking when he said that the job of the
> president was not to represent the elite but to represent
> those people who don't have representatives, the poor and
> the underclass and the minorities. Those are generally the
> sides and the issues that we stand along with. There are
> thousands of registered lobbyists in Washington who
> represent those who can afford them; that is the elite. But
> that's not the religious community's role. Our role is to
> combat [the elites].[20]

Although they did not identify directly with "the poor,"
conservatives shared a populist perspective with liberals
and saw themselves as representatives of a nonelite constituency. Since conservative Christian lobbyists are usually
aligned with the Republican party, many observers mis-
takenly conclude that they share the more wealthy socioeconomic characteristics of the Republican party. Richard

Viguerie, the direct-mail genius of both secular and Christian conservative activists, debunked this myth. He stated:

> You may notice a missing element here: big business. I'd like to say something here about the so-called support for conservative causes by business. As far as the New Right is concerned, it never existed. It is not true that what is good for General Motors is good for the country—or what is good for big business is automatically good for conservatives. The New Right rejects both propositions. This is one of the things that distinguishes us from the Republican establishment.[21]

From the perspective of conservative Christians, Matthew Smyth of Christian Voice stated, "Our membership is not wealthy. They are not the elite. They are average, middle American people who go to church on Sunday and work a forty-hour week. We have a lot of elderly as members and many blue-collar workers."[22] A lobbyist for the Moral Majority identified this same constituency in distinctively populist terms.

> Our average contribution is $12–15 by thousands of people across this country who work every day. They bale hay; they wash cars and drive taxis. We see ourselves representing the small man in Washington. We, the small guys, had to elbow and push and shove to get our way to the table. There are still the big guys that try to intimidate us, . . . but we are a powerhouse because of the people, we are a powerhouse because of our love for God. We are a powerhouse because we love America. That's our power.[23]

The populist perspective of religious lobbyists seems deeply rooted in the religious tradition. At the heart of all religious faiths is the conviction that the relationship between God and humans is primary; nothing else matters. No worldly institution or power can supersede this relationship. Elites, in their own way, have power and prestige that can even rival the power of God. Elites are often vene-rated—even worshiped. Some religions provide a theologi-cal veneer for this adoration, but prophetic religion pro-vides an alternative power, the power of God. This religion provides the impetus to reject the "principalities and powers" of this world. Religious faith can provide stan-dards by which to judge worldly powers. When worldly elites fail to uphold these standards, religious activists sound the call to battle.

THE PROPHETIC BATTLE AGAINST DIFFERENT ELITES: THE WEALTHY AND THE SECULAR

While liberals and conservatives both claim to challenge an elite, they see different elites in control. Liberal groups work against the dominance of wealthy elites. Conserva-tives work against a secular elite. Liberals are driven by the sense that the resources of society are directed away from the needs of the poor and toward the wealthy. Before the end of the Cold War, the dominance of the military-indus-trial complex was a big concern. Now a more general cor-porate power structure is feared. Conservatives do not share this concern about the power of the wealthy or the military-industrial complex. Though not usually allied di-rectly with big business or other corporate interests, reli-gious conservatives often support lower taxes and in-creased military spending, which are at the core of the corporate policy agenda. In contrast to liberals, they fear a different elite; they feel that a dominant secular elite is con-trolling the country. That elite refuses to protect the rights of the unborn or permit prayer in the schools. This secular elite refuses to make necessary moral judgments about the sexual preferences of citizens or the content of sex educa-tion programs in public schools.

A Moral Majority brochure declares that its members are

"sick and tired of the way many amoral and secular humanists and other liberals are destroying the traditional family and moral values on which our nation was built."[24] Conservatives believe that the secular elites of Washington do not understand and therefore cannot speak for moral values and the family. One new group organized around concern for the family is the Family Research Council. The executive director is Gary Bauer, former director of domestic policy issues for the Reagan administration. In an interview, Bauer said:

> There's no scarcity of high-paid attorneys representing big business or big labor or all the other interest groups here in town. But there's been a vacuum when it comes to lobbyists who speak for the American family. I hope we can fill that void.[25]

Matthew Smyth echoed this judgment. He expressed his members' objection to the primary principles of Washington politics.

> Our constituency is upset about the dominant trend of public policy. They are concerned about sex education with no value base. They are concerned about schools that don't start their day with prayer. They are concerned with politicians who can condone the murdering of the unborn with no sense of moral contradiction.[26]

The Reagan years revealed something about the nature of the conservative groups. In the early 1980s, the religious right gained unprecedented access to the inner circles of power. Seen as a central reason for Reagan's victory, they seemingly were a part of the power elite. But President Reagan gave more attention to economic issues than the social issues of the Christian right. At the end of the Reagan and Bush years, many conservative Christians felt betrayed by the White House.[27] They could have compromised their views to maintain their position of power. With some exceptions, few chose that option. Jerry Falwell's endorsement of George Bush in 1988, when more conservative candidates were running, is one example of compromise. Yet the dominant trend among conservatives has been a retreat from Washington.[28] Finding the national arena hostile to their policies, many have increasingly pressed their concerns at the state and local levels. Jerry Falwell himself closed his organization and left Washington. Gary Bauer stayed in Washington, but he resigned from a position in the Reagan administration to become executive director of the Family Research Council. There he engaged in harsh criticism of the Bush administration. Pat Robertson formed a new organization, the Christian Coalition, located outside of Washington, with a strong state and local agenda.

Analyzing such moves, some concluded that the ascendancy of the Christian right is over.[29] Steve Bruce argues that the failure of the Christian right to transform society may lead it to a new strategy of "claiming social space for its beliefs, values, and practices on the grounds that it represents a legitimate minority which the modern state discriminates against."[30] This prediction may come true, but fundamentalists are still aggressively involved in politics. Some organizations, such as the Christian Coalition, focus on state and local politics because they have a greater chance of winning at that level. Ralph Reed, the organization's executive director, said, "We tried to change Washington when we should have been focusing on the states."[31] The Pennsylvania Christian Coalition, for example, has distributed a county action plan offering advice to fundamentalists. The plan advises winning power in the local Republican party and then working to affect state and national politics. That strategy is repeated all across the country.[32] The battle against secular humanist elites remains intense; only the venue has changed.

Though not retreating from Washington, liberal lobbyists express a similar sense of distance and alienation from

Washington insiders. Robert Tiller of the American Baptist Church acknowledged the outsider status of religious lobbyists. He said, "There are literally tens of thousands of lobbyists in Washington, and I don't know what most of them are doing. I don't know whom they represent, what they are up to. I don't bump into them. . . . My sense is that an accurate generalization is that they represent the elite, those who can afford lobbyists and lawyers."[33] While many political analysts see social relationships as an indispensable part of building influence,[34] religious lobbyists seem to shun them. A few religious lobbyists were frank enough to admit that they were not a part of the Washington social scene. Undoubtedly, this isolation prevents them from engaging in some of the wheeling and dealing, the forming of alliances and compromises, that take place in the Washington social circuit. According to John Carr of the U.S. Catholic Conference,

> We tend not to be an organization that plays the Washington game. We do not do the social circuit; we do not do the conventions or lobbying parties. You will not find us with a lot of shrimp or roast beef up there. It's just not our style.[35]

Because of their discontent with the Washington establishment, some lobbyists called for a more full-scale challenge of it. One liberal lobbyist spoke of dreams to establish a religious political party that would challenge the priorities of both parties.[36] Some conservatives called for changing of the guard in Congress. A 1988 article in a Moral Majority publication, *Liberty Report*, was entitled, "Does America Need a New Congress?" In a cutting indictment, the authors argued, "Some of the most radical bills ever written crossed congressional desks last year, reminding us that the fight for traditional family values, religious freedom and responsible government never ends." Decrying congressional action on issues of civil rights, gay rights, foreign aid, defense spending, and abortion, they called for a new Congress.[37] In a similar manner, a central dimension of Pat Robertson's Christian Coalition is the belief that achieving an "orderly and progressive society" requires citizens to elect to public office Christians who will promote traditional values.[38]

At a time when anti-Washington sentiment seems to be at an all-time high, religious lobbyists may have tapped a surging vein of public sentiment. Campaigning against Washington is increasingly fashionable. Citizens seem to believe that the problems of the United States stem from the errors of our Washington politicians; they feel that major changes are necessary. The 1992 campaign of Ross Perot is a prime example. He painted a picture of a Capitol awash with special interest legislators and lobbyists who trade large campaign contributions for legislation that undermines the broader public. With such rhetoric, Perot became a viable presidential candidate as an independent.

Because Perot appeared suddenly on the national scene, many accuse him of opportunism. In contrast, religious lobbyists have been declaring their criticisms of Washington politicians even when it was out of fashion. This history shows the greater sincerity and depth of their convictions. Religious lobbyists' actions stem from beliefs that have long been at the center of their faith. They are not recent converts to the politics of criticizing the Washington establishment.[39]

When religious lobbyists indict the system so scathingly, they are acting as independent centers of power. This is a role that organized religion has often assumed—precisely because it is religious. Stephen Carter stated in a recent book that the United States trivializes religion and seeks to deny it a position as an autonomous power center in public life. True religion, says Carter, "speaks to its members in a voice different from that of the state, and when the voice moves the faithful to action, a religion may act as a counter-weight to the authority of the state."[40] Carter cites John Courtney Murray, a Catholic theologian and church leader, who said the appropriate question was not "whether Catholicism is compatible with American democracy," but rather "whether American democracy is compatible with Catholicism."[41] Understood this way, religion will challenge elite values deemed unjust. Different religions will then challenge slavery, apartheid, the military, feminists, gays . . . the list goes on. Instead of following the elite, religion moves to the beat of a different drummer.

THE PROPHETIC VISION OF RELIGIOUS LOBBYISTS

Like prophets of old, religious lobbyists do more than disparage Washington politics. They also proclaim a vision of a new political reality. Not limiting themselves to a narrow agenda, they usually express a desire for fundamental change. Most secular lobbyists are more narrow.[42] Arthur Keys, director of an ecumenical advocacy group said, "Our goal is to help bring about a more just world."[43] Another liberal lobby's goal is to work "for a just, caring and peaceful society."[44] The Presbyterian Church states that its Washington office helps "the people of God press themselves and the world in the direction of the Kingdom of God that is coming."[45]

All three Catholic organizations expressed broad goals; they made no reference to changing a narrowly defined policy. Nancy Sylvester of NETWORK, a Catholic citizens lobby, says that her organization "seeks structural change through the legislative process."[46] A quote on the cover of a brochure written by Catholic Charities states, "Action on behalf of justice and participation in the transformation of the world appear to us as a constitutive dimension of the

preaching of the Gospel or the Church's mission for the re-
demption of the human race."[47] Similarly, a lobbyist for the
U.S. Catholic Conference stated:

> Christians believe that Jesus' commandment to love one's
> neighbor should extend beyond individual relationships to
> infuse and transform all human relations from the family
> to the entire human community. . . . [This commandment]
> requires both individual acts of charity and concern and
> understanding and action on a broader scale in pursuit of
> peace and in opposition to poverty, hunger, and injustice.
> Such action necessarily involves the institutions and
> structures of society, the economy, and politics.[48]

For conservatives, a brochure published by Concerned
Women for America invited members to do nothing less
than "Come Help Save America."[49] To save America, conservatives are concerned with the preservation of traditional values. Of particular concern are "family values" and
the wide array of legislation that affects the family. The legislative director of Concerned Women for America expressed this concern more fully.

> The most basic reason for the existence of Concerned
> Women for America is to preserve and protect the
> traditional American family through Judeo-Christian
> values. We are concerned with those forces which tend to
> weaken the traditional family. . . . We are looking to
> preserve the existing laws that we consider to be
> compatible with our values which are Biblically based and
> then trying to expose the new trends or movements that
> come along that would make it difficult for those who
> want to hold those values and continue to keep them.[50]

Gary Bauer of the Family Research Council stated, "We are
devoted to strengthening the family and the Judeo-Christian values that serve as the foundation of our society."[51]

Religious lobbyists express their sweeping goals with
clear calls to reorder the existing priorities of government.
NETWORK commits "to fight for reordering of our nation's

budget priorities."[52] The Religious Task Force for Central America works "for justice and peace in Central America, and towards changing the policy priorities of our government towards the region."[53] Generally, there was a conviction that national problems could be solved if the political agenda were reoriented to reflect religious values. The director of IMPACT, a liberal ecumenical lobby, spoke of the potentially far-reaching significance of religious lobbying. Recalling her organization's origins, she stated a conviction that religious lobbying could contribute nothing less than solutions to the major social problems of America.

> IMPACT was founded after the destruction of Washington and the riots in '68. A group of folks from Jewish, Roman Catholic, and Protestant communities were sitting as Washington was burning. They were holding their heads in their hands saying if the religious community had only been able to really get together and address the kind of social ills that produced the kind of discrimination that we saw rampant in this country and the hatred that resulted in King's death, if we had only been able to get our act together and set aside our differences and find our points of continuity, we could have changed the course of public policy, and the kind of brutality and violence that had just destroyed this city might not have had to happen.[54]

Religious lobbyists seek to fundamentally transform the political and social reality of America. These sweeping goals are rooted in a religious understanding of the achievement of the kingdom of God on earth.[55] James Matlack of the American Friends Service Committee expressed the implications of this concept for lobbying:

> I come at that question in a somewhat larger context in that the ultimate goal of the American Friends Service Committee would not be achieved short of the coming of the kingdom or some equivalent of a world order of peace and justice, and sufficiency and stability for all peoples. We work for an idealistic level which is always beyond

historical completion, I suspect, though we'd better get
closer than we are, or else history may do us in.[56]

The Mennonites also made use of the concept of the kingdom of God. Like the Friends, they articulated the tension
between contemporary politics and the impossible goals of
the kingdom of God, but they felt the imperative to work
for those goals nonetheless.

> While the government cannot be expected to live by
> Kingdom [of God] norms, far greater constraint in reliance
> on military force is not an unrealistic request. The
> prevalent assumption is that international affairs can only
> succeed if armed force or the threat of its use is the
> principal engine driving U.S. foreign policy. We believe
> this assumption can be appropriately challenged by the
> religious community.[57]

The goals of religious lobbyists are consistent with their
pervasive sense of discontent. In the face of a political
world that seems riddled with compromise and impurity,
the religious lobbyists call for comprehensive transformation. To do less would be to approve tacitly a system they
find morally objectionable. Religious lobbyists are unwilling to play the political game as it is traditionally played.
Whereas most lobbyists seek small changes in a narrow
policy arena, religious lobbyists seek large changes to make
America and even the world more consistent with their religious principles.

THE PROPHETIC ISSUE AGENDA

The grand vision of religious lobbyists translates into a
packed agenda of legislative concerns. Religious lobbyists
focus on more issues than their secular counterparts. In a
broad survey of representatives in Washington, Robert Nelson and his associates found that representatives spend

time in four to six policy areas.[58] In contrast, religious lobbyists focused their energy on a minimum of six issues and
a maximum of twenty-four. This characterization of religious lobbyists also contrasts with Heclo's description of
the policy process as a series of "issue networks," which are
communities of policy experts who work on one issue.[59]

The Catholic organization NETWORK shows the breadth
of its concerns when it claims to influence members of
Congress to enact laws providing economic justice for the
poor and the powerless, protecting human rights at home
and abroad, promoting disarmament, and ensuring world
peace.[60] Expressing a similarly extensive range of concerns,
Interfaith Action for Economic Justice has an issue agenda
that "works to secure just and effective food and agriculture, health and human services, and development and economic policies for the world's poor and hungry."[61]

In their issue agendas, there is a fair amount of unanimity among liberal and among conservative groups. Among
liberal groups, that unanimity is facilitated by the existence
of several coalitions that have a long history of working
together. Interfaith IMPACT for Justice and Peace, the National Council of Churches, and the Washington Inter-
religious Staff Council are all organizations in which Jewish, Protestant, and Catholic organizations cooperate in
their lobbying efforts. While not completely unanimous,
lobbyists representing these diverse theological traditions
agree on most issues.[62]

Not all organized religious interests have a multi-issue
agenda. The Religious Coalition for Central America, as its
name indicates, focuses only on issues that relate to this
region. Bread for the World limits itself to antipoverty legislation but is also involved in legislation concerning foreign
aid and military spending. Even their foreign policy interests, however, are related to their interest in alleviating
poverty. A recent significant effort involved an attempt to
redirect budgetary resources from military spending to an-

tipoverty programs. Bread for the World sought to cut military spending in half. Symbolizing their work, these lobbyists called their campaign the Harvest of Peace.[63]

Only three groups devote themselves exclusively to issues concerning the separation of church and state. These groups include the Baptist Joint Committee for Public Affairs, the Washington Office of the Seventh Day Adventists, and Americans United for the Separation of Church and State. Their sole focus on issues of religious freedom and the separation of church and state made these three organizations distinct from the other organized religious interests in this study. Stan Hastey of the Baptist Joint Committee stated, "We see ourselves in a tradition going back to Roger Williams. We seek to promote issues relating to what Williams called soul liberty."[64] Their issue agenda included opposition to school prayer, public funding for church-sponsored child care, and tuition tax credits. Because their focus is narrow, their coalition partners are unpredictable. They join liberal groups in opposing school prayer and tuition tax credits. But they part company with some of the same liberal groups in opposing efforts to expand day-care programs, particularly when legislation included any government aid to church-operated centers.

The remaining groups are not so limited in focus. They worked in a number of issue areas including foreign policy, social policy, environmental policy, and civil rights. In the area of foreign policy, nearly all the liberal groups supported sanctions against South Africa until African National Congress leader Nelson Mandela called for their end. Until that moment in the fall of 1993, South African sanctions had been a major priority of liberal groups. In addition, opposing Reagan administration efforts to aid the Nicaraguan Contras consumed the liberal lobbies until the Sandinista government fell from power in the 1990 elections. At that point the Contras ended their struggle and the issue was moot. Other defense issues have included opposition to military aid, support of the INF treaty, and opposition to funding for the MX missile and the Strategic Defense Initiative. These specific issues are consistent with liberal goals of peace and disarmament. A statement from a Mennonite brochure summarizes the foreign policy agenda of politically liberal religious organizations. The brochure states that the Mennonites sought to promote

> constructive alternatives [that] include: (1) a more energetic and creative use of diplomacy, (2) rectifying global economic disparities, (3) the undergirding rather than undermining of international law, (4) greater use of U.N. Peacekeeping forces in areas of persistent violence, (5) seeing the world's problems from a South-North (poor-rich) perspective, not just from an East-West perspective.[65]

In domestic policy, liberal groups worked to support increased funding for child care and increases in the minimum wage. In addition, aid to the homeless and the Family and Medical Leave Act both received considerable support from liberal groups in the last few congressional sessions. Since Bill Clinton's election, liberal lobbyists have supported many Clinton administration initiatives including gun control, increased funding for Head Start, and the Earned Income Tax Credit. But they have opposed Clinton's efforts to expand the death penalty and curtail welfare benefits after two years. In addition, they have generally positioned themselves to the left of President Clinton's health care initiatives. They are more supportive of single-payer plans.

In the area of civil liberties and civil rights, liberal religious interests devoted considerable energy to the successful passage of the civil rights bills of 1987 and 1991. In addition, many groups worked on the Hate Crime Statistics Act, the genocide treaty, and legislation focusing on the redress of Japanese citizens. In 1993 religious lobbies of all political persuasions joined together to support the Religious Freedom Restoration Act. This legislation was written to counteract a 1990 Supreme Court decision that granted more power to government to restrict religion. Congress passed the bill by decisive margins and President Clinton signed the legislation in November of 1993.[66]

Unanimity is frequent, but there are exceptions. Protestant and Catholic groups do not usually share the Jewish groups' commitment to aid to Israel. Even so, their disagreements do not prevent them from working together on the remainder of their issue agenda. Liberal lobbyists also disagreed on abortion. Because of the real split on this issue, liberal religious lobbying in favor of abortion rights is sporadic and often seemingly halfhearted. The Roman Catholic Church, which actively pursues its prolife position on abortion, is much more active on this issue. Uniquely, the Catholic Church pursues a liberal agenda on virtually every other issue besides abortion.

Conservative groups also have a broad agenda, but they have two priority issues: abortion and school prayer. They have also focused on tuition tax credits and gay rights. In the last two years, the Christian Coalition has tried to expand its concern to economic issues. The 1994 legislative voting record published by the organization indicates opposition to the Clinton Stimulus Package, the overall Clinton budget bill, and the Clinton health plan. Generally, the Christian Coalition has opposed both increased taxation and spending. Beyond fiscal policy, Ralph Reed, the executive director, attempted to involve the organization in the NAFTA debate. Despite these forays, there is little evidence that economic issues will displace social issues as the predominant concerns of conservative Christian activists.

Academic research suggests that lobbyists are more successful when they narrow their focus. In his study of Washington lobbying, William Browne finds that most contemporary interest groups seek to narrow their focus and limit confrontations with other organized interests. This strategy is intended to preserve a narrower process of elite accommodation. In general, he concluded that organizations with a smaller agenda were more successful. Over a three-year period, they were better able to achieve tangible legislative success. In addition, legislators, administrative personnel, and lobbyists were asked to judge the influence of 136 groups and rated those with the narrower focus as more influential.[67] If Browne's research is correct, religious lobbyists' ability to influence legislation will decline because of their broad agendas.

THE PURISM OF PROPHETIC LOBBYING

In pursuing a multi-issue agenda, religious lobbyists are similar to "amateur" or "purist" party activists. These activists arose to challenge the views and status of the political machines in cities throughout the United States.[68] Like religious critics of the Washington elite, party amateurs were driven by the sense that party leaders or bosses ruled the party in an undemocratic and even corrupt fashion. To describe those who challenged party bosses, the term "amateur" was chosen carefully. It does not mean someone who is inept or lacking in skills. Indeed, the amateurs defeated the so-called professional politicians and took over a number of party organizations. Rather, "an amateur is one who finds politics intrinsically interesting because it expresses a conception of the public interest." An amateur thinks of politics more as a way to advance principles and less as a way to elect people. While professional party activists seek pragmatic compromises necessary for electoral victory, amateur activists would rather engage in principled attention to political issues.[69]

Many amateur party activists had little previous experience in party politics. Often, their goal was to transform party organizations that they viewed as corrupt. Similarly, the amateur status of religious lobbyists is defined in part by their previous experience in government. Though it is possible to maintain an amateur outlook when working in government, most activists get increasingly pragmatic after gaining experience in government. As stated earlier, few religious lobbyists have prior experience in either appointed or elective office. Their work as a religious lobbyist was for many their first political job. Table 10 compares my universe of lobbyists with the larger universe of lobbyists as recorded in the studies of Schlozman and Tierney, Milbrath, Salisbury, Berry, and Zwier.

In contrast to religious interest groups, most secular organizations regularly hire former government officials to

TABLE 10
Lobbyists with Prior Experience in Government

CATEGORY (AND SOURCE)	PERCENTAGE
All lobbyists (Schlozman and Tierney, 1986)	86
All lobbyists (Milbrath, 1963)	56
All lobbyists (Salisbury, 1986)	54
Public interest lobbyists (Berry, 1977)	26
Religious lobbyists*	9
Religious lobbyists (Zwier, 1988)	6

Sources: Robert H. Salisbury, "Washington Lobbyists: A Collective Portrait," in *Interest Group Politics*, 2nd ed. Allan J. Cigler and Burdett A. Loomis (Washington, DC: CQ Press, 1986); Lester W. Milbrath, *The Washington Lobbyists* (Chicago: Rand McNally, 1963); Kay Lehman Schlozman and John T. Tierney, *Organized Interests and American Democracy* (New York: Harper & Row, 1986); Jeffrey M. Berry, *Lobbying for the People: The Political Behavior of Public Interest Groups* (Princeton, NJ: Princeton University Press, 1977); Robert Zwier, "The World and Worldview of Religious Lobbyists," paper presented at the 1988 convention of the Midwest Political Science Association, Chicago.

*My estimate of the percent of religious lobbyists may underestimate the actual amount. I did not ask lobbyists directly about their government experience. I only asked them about their background prior to assuming their present job. Only three mentioned government experience. A few may have had such experience but failed to mention it in reply to my open-ended question. The Zwier study provides a more accurate estimate.

lobby for them. Scholars have assessed this flow of personnel and termed it a revolving door.[70] Hiring former government officials is virtually unknown among religious lobbyists. Only 6–9 percent of religious lobbyists had any
previous experience in government. Most of the religious
lobbyists had prior experience in church work, education,
business, or state-level religious lobbies. Some are ordained
ministers, and this fact affects their work. Religious lobbyists seem to view their work more as an opportunity to
make moral pronouncements. To many, the articulation of
moral principles seems more important than specific legislative victories. This tendency varied among the different
lobbyists.

Religious organizations could choose a different path in
recruiting their staff. They could hire former government
officials to lobby for their organization, but they almost
never do. Surely there are many members of religious communities who work in different parts of government, but
religious organizations make no effort to recruit them.
Many former members of Congress are active in their
churches, yet none take jobs as religious lobbyists. If organized religious interests hired former government officials
to represent them, the style of religious lobbying would
change dramatically. Because these lobbyists would have
spent more of their career in Washington, they would be
less critical of the Washington establishment. They would
have friends and contacts with whom to share information
and socialize. They would possess more technical expertise
and might be more willing to compromise.

One conservative lobbyist admitted his own naivete and
the inexperience of his colleagues. Though he claimed increased expertise after years of work as a lobbyist, he discussed the early days when representatives of the Christian
right did not know even the most basic parts of the political
process.

> When we began our organization twelve years ago, we
> had many questions. What's a politician? Who's a
> congressman? What's a senator? What's a primary? What's
> a caucus? These were all part of a language or a culture
> that was so foreign to those of us who were committed to
> prayer, to the study of scripture, to working with our
> hands.[71]

Undoubtedly, this lack of experience may exacerbate the
tendency of religious lobbyists to focus on broad principles
rather than legislative details. Some religious lobbyists get
shrewdly involved in the intricacies of legislation, but they
seem to be the exceptions. The dominant approach seems to
be an amateur style of principled pronouncements from on
high. In his book on religious lobbying, Allen Hertzke
wrote, "A number of congressional aides felt that religious
lobbyists, or many of them, face a unique psychological im-
pediment to mastering the details of the legislative process. . . . It is this prophetic temptation that can keep the
religious mind from focusing on the mundane details of the
legislative process."[72] The consequences are that religious
lobbyists are often not a part of the final preparation of
bills. This failing is evident in a religious lobbyist's reaction
to the final drafting of the 1985 farm bill.

> In the early stages of committee deliberation, all sorts of
> groups were invited to provide testimony and many
> focused on such foundational issues as property rights,
> stewardship, justice, and so forth. But when the crunch
> time came and legislators needed to find majorities for
> specific sections of the bill, they called on interest groups
> who stood to gain or lose some material benefits rather
> than the groups who had articulated a more philosophical
> approach to public policy. Finer points of morality and
> ethics got lost in the struggle to fashion compromises
> acceptable to specific constituencies.[73]

In the end, when legislators craft the nuances of legislation,
it is sometimes hard to know whether religious lobbyists

have left an impression or influenced the bills at all. On certain pieces of legislation, they surely have, but heralding values is often their most important contribution.

PROPHETIC DEFINITIONS OF SUCCESS

Not unexpectedly, religious lobbyists define success differently than other lobbyists. In response to a question asking them to state their definition of effectiveness, religious lobbyists redefined the term. In contrast to a narrow focus on winning or losing, they proclaimed devotion to principle as their main purpose. One pamphlet included this exhortation:

> Rather, we are called by our God to act . . . to act boldly for justice and compassion whatever the odds. . . . For the men and women of IMPACT today is not a time to retreat. Social justice may no longer be a fashionable concept. But, justice and empathy are not fads. They are a matter of faith. And, a matter of action.[74]

The religious community in Washington holds protracted debates about the ethics of compromising, and many religious lobbyists argue that winning is not the most important outcome of their work. One lobbyist expressed frustration that so much time was spent on this discussion. This person lamented that some so-called strategy sessions were consumed by this topic.[75]

There is a sense that religious lobbyists want to preach as much as they seek to lobby. When asked, "In the context of Washington, D.C., what does it mean to be effective?" three-fourths of the respondents talked about the importance of articulating their message over and above the importance of winning or losing on specific pieces of legislation. This question was worded in the least leading and most general way possible. Alternatively, one could have asked whether it is better to be faithful than successful. This phrasing would have elicited a particular response. Instead, the question was worded in an open-ended way. Nonetheless, most of the religious lobbyists favored stating principles over and above passing specific pieces of legislation. This attitude contrasts with that of most Washington lobbyists. John Carr, who works for the U.S. Catholic Conference, stated this position most clearly.

> To be effective in Washington means to contribute to campaigns; it means to make a difference in the next week. For us, that is theologically and pastorally inappropriate. . . . For us to be effective is to be clear about our values, to be consistent in advocating those values, and to offer not just principles but as much as possible a constituency that believes in those principles.[76]

Many lobbyists spoke in terms of long-term rather than short-term success. The Presbyterian lobbyist Mary Jane Patterson expressed her intent to advocate faithfully a concern even when it falls off the official agenda. She contends that the advocacy of unfashionable positions is the special vocation of the church. No one else will do this. Before Bill Clinton was even a declared presidential candidate, she spoke prophetically about her calling to maintain a focus on health care. Even though Presidents Reagan and Bush did not seem interested, she persevered.

> To be effective is to be faithful. In the language of the streets, this means stick-to-itiveness. When I first came here, I had health care in my portfolio. The Presbyterian Church believes in health care for all Americans. Presidential administrations and Congress have dropped their support of health care. But now it will come again in the 101st or 102nd Congress. Whether it's four years from now or forty, we are going to get health care for all Americans. So it would seem to me that faithfulness means that you stick with your principle. The Presbyterian Church is not likely to change its stand on the fact that we believe in health care for all Americans.[77]

Similarly, the editor of a Lutheran denominational magazine, Edgar Trexler, acknowledged that churches often take unpopular stands. They are accused of being naive, but in the long run prove to be brilliantly foresighted.

> Churches which study the human and moral dimensions of
> . . . issues are often criticized as not having sufficient
> expertise to make such a pronouncement. Yet almost
> uncannily, political forces often move years later in
> directions suggested earlier by churches.[78]

Patterson's continual concern about health care is evidence of this trend. Trexler pointed to additional examples of prophetic concern. He stated that in 1958 the National Council of Churches called for recognition of the People's Republic of China, which finally took place twenty years later. In 1965 it advocated the negotiation of a cease-fire in Vietnam. A decade later this finally occurred. Finally, Trexler notes that the Lutheran Church called for an end to South Africa's occupation of Namibia in 1978; the occupation ended in 1989. Similarly, the potential for short-term failure and long-term success was extolled by Gretchen Eick, a long-term religious lobbyist in Washington. She stated,

> From the beginning of the Judaic-Christian story, God has
> been propelling human beings into the political arena. And
> human beings have responded to this risky call and have
> confronted powers and principalities, sometimes
> experiencing embarrassment and dramatic failure *at least
> initially.* . . . In striving to be faithful . . . we, like Jonah may
> find ourselves feeling exposed and made a fool by God's
> compassion for the world and its people. [emphasis added][79]

Lobbyists who share this prophetic perspective may not hold an impressive annual scorecard of wins and losses. John Lillie, acting director of the lobbying office of the Evangelical Lutheran Church of America, stated,

> If you were to list the issues in a column that we are
> working on and count how many of those passed or how

> many of those end up the way the way we advocated, we
> probably would not be judged very effective. But I would
> hope that our effectiveness is judged by establishing the
> integrity of this office.[80]

Outside of mainline Protestantism, other lobbyists reiter-
ated this perspective. A representative of the National Association of Evangelicals spoke about a concern beyond the
outcome of specific bills.

> I think it [effectiveness] means foremost the articulation of
> the evangelical message in the Washington environment.
> This is not drafting legislation only, or playing the insider
> role on the hill the way some groups do. . . . Effectiveness
> is involvement not in specific policy prescriptions, but
> often in articulating principles in the process. That's how
> the church ought to be judged in the Washington arena,
> not by whether we've won or lost but by the degree to
> which we are effectively able to influence society on the
> moral values which we believe in.[81]

Interestingly, the major exceptions to this amateurish definition of effectiveness were the three Jewish lobbyists and
the conservative Christian lobbyists. Each Jewish lobbyist
stated clearly that winning specific legislative victories was
his or her first priority. David Harris of the American Jewish
Congress said that effectiveness means "to see the things
you want enacted or not enacted as the case may be."[82] Similarly, Glen Stein of the Union of American Hebrew Congregations said that effectiveness means "getting the legislation you support passed and the legislation you oppose
defeated."[83] When asked directly, these lobbyists did concur
with the value of a faithful articulation of principles, but
unlike other religious lobbyists, they expressed clear limits
to that strategy.

> I think there are certainly times when the role of an
> organization is to stake out one end of the spectrum and to
> stand fast—to mark off a boundary on the playing field, if
> you will. On the other hand, if all you are doing is

standing out there pretending like you are a sideline, you are not really being a part of the process. And then you are not quite as effective as you could be.[84]

This concern about specific legislative accomplishments and failures was a minority perspective among religious lobbyists. Non-Jewish lobbyists were more stalwart in a definition of success as faithfulness, not necessarily as legislative gains.

The three largest conservative organizations seem also to take winning more seriously. The Family Research Council, a think tank and advocacy organization, has a large budget and membership. Concerned Women of America has drawn many accolades for its lobbying prowess. The Christian Coalition is showing surges of strength. All three organizations generally combine a refusal to compromise with a tenacious focus on winning. All have developed a very sophisticated ability to generate grassroots pressure on elected officials. The Christian Coalition has also been active in electoral politics and has demonstrated an ability to mobilize voters in decisive numbers. Yet these efforts to play political hardball seem to be the exception among religious lobbyists, who seem most concerned about the purity of their message.

Such a perspective is rare in Washington. Most secular lobbyists focus on specific material gains and are indifferent to clearly stating their principles. Religious lobbyists seem unable to take this approach. Instead, they adopt a style that seems distinctly unsuitable for conventional victories. They advocate an exceedingly broad agenda; they show less interest in detail; they eschew hiring staff with Washington experience. They seem to seek success on their own terms. They seek and proclaim the need for radical transformation. If they ever are successful in actually achieving that, the political world will have changed tremendously. In the meantime, their tangible successes seem slight, but they have adapted to Washington by adopting a pattern of tactics that will be described in the next chapter.

6
CHAPTER

The Tactics of Prophetic Lobbying

All lobbyists choose from two broad categories of tactics to achieve their goals: outsider lobbying and insider lobbying. Outsider lobbying involves cultivating grassroots or constituency pressure on elected officials. Insider lobbying involves helping to draft legislation and shape the implementation of policy. Insider lobbying usually involves a long-term relationship with government officials. Its venue is inside, not outside, the beltway of Washington, D.C. Its style is quiet negotiation and persuasion between old friends. Routinely, insider lobbying involves an office meeting in which pending legislation is discussed. Additional sites include golf courses, restaurants, Washington cocktail parties, and association meetings all across the United States.

In its purest form, insider lobbying is practiced by the lobbying superstars, political professionals who have reached the pinnacle of the lobbying profession. Veteran Washington watcher Hedrick Smith writes:

> Their game thrives on the clubbiness of the old-boy network. It turns on the camaraderie of personal friendships, on expertise born of experience. It taps old loyalties and well-practiced access. It draws on the common bond of old battles and the certain knowledge

that you may lose on this year's tax bill, but you'll be back
to revise it next year, and that yesterday's foe may be
tomorrow's ally. It depends on relationships for the long
haul.[1]

These insiders are people like Thomas Boggs, Clark Clifford, or Birch Bayh who command influence developed over
a long tenure in Washington.[2] Many, like Bayh and Clifford,
are former government officials. Their previous public service gives them the insider's access that is invaluable to
their subsequent lobbying career.

As noted in the previous chapter, no religious lobbyists
are former elected officials, but some religious lobbyists do
have insider access. Hyman Bookbinder of the American
Jewish Committee and Ed Snyder, who lobbied for the Friends
Committee on National Legislation, are often mentioned as
religious lobbyists who enjoy insider access.[3] In 1988, Bookbinder left the American Jewish Committee to work in the
presidential campaign of Michael Dukakis. But this close relationship between lobbyists and government officials seems to
be the exception. The rarity of such relationships reveals religious lobbyists' disinterest in the insider game.

The stereotype of insider lobbying is the exchange of a
campaign contribution for a vote on a bill or a regulatory
revision. Certainly, money is a crucial resource of the lobbyist, but the path of influence is usually not as straightfor-
ward as the backroom quid pro quo. More than a direct
trade for a vote, a campaign contribution buys access. With
access to government officials, the insider lobbyist is able to
develop a relationship. Members of Congress return insider
lobbyists' phone calls and honor their requests for meetings. Since most religious lobbyists are not affiliated with a
political action committee, they are handicapped by their
inability to trade access for campaign contributions. Veteran religious lobbyist Ed Snyder notes a decline in the ability of religious lobbyists to gain access.

> There are so many organizations giving money to members
> of Congress to buy access that by the time the appointment
> secretary schedules those people to talk to the members
> directly, there doesn't seem to be much time left to talk
> with people from organizations that have not made those
> kinds of contributions. In my thirty years of experience, I
> can see a very definite change for the worse in terms of
> gaining access to members directly. It's absolutely harder
> for our kind of organization to get an appointment.[4]

For insider lobbying, this access to government officials
is crucial because it can enable lobbyists to provide their
own perspective and information to legislators, which can
change the shape of legislation. This exchange is the insider
lobbyist's most important function; legislators rely on it as
well. Because they have to vote on thousands of bills on a
myriad of different subjects, legislators often need to turn to
lobbyists for necessary, albeit biased, information to help
them vote. Lobbyists are usually experts on the legislation
for which they lobby; they usually know more than the legislators. They also may know enough about a legislator's
constituency to enable them to advise legislators how to explain their vote to their constituency.[5] Alternatively, a legislator's constituents may have little direct concern about certain votes. On these low-salience issues, legislators can vote
according to lobbyists' wishes with no fear of electoral consequences. In these cases, a campaign contribution may
have great influence. All of these situations offer insider
lobbyists the opportunity to wield great power.

In contrast to insider lobbying, outsider lobbying involves the broader public in the legislative process.
Whereas insider lobbying operates inside the beltway, outsider lobbying makes contact with constituents outside the
nation's capital. Whereas insider lobbying trades information and collegial persuasion, outsider lobbying transforms
public opinion and generates constituency pressure. Where

the resources of insider lobbying are information and money, the currency of outsider lobbying is constituency opinion and votes. Effective outsider lobbying arouses the citizenry to express its concerns.

All lobbyists, including religious lobbyists, use a mix of insider and outsider lobbying. In recent years, most Washington observers have concluded that insider lobbying without outsider support is largely ineffective. Many lobbyists who previously worked exclusively on the inside are developing a sophisticated ability to generate grassroots pressure on government officials. Many corporations are hiring firms that enable them to generate thousands of letters on any issue. They make use of high-tech methods like fax machines and satellite video networks. In some cases, lobbying organizations invite calls to their 800 number and then transfer their calls directly to a congressional office.[6] They are so effective at targeting specific slices of the electorate that many argue that their grassroots mobilization amounts to a kind of "AstroTurf" campaign.[7] The grassroots support that they generate is really an artificial exaggeration of the true views of the electorate.

While most lobbyists use an outsider strategy, religious lobbyists use it more exclusively. To be sure, religious lobbyists use insider tactics, but they use them less frequently than other lobbyists. Furthermore, they do not combine a grassroots strategy with the insider tactics that are the stock in trade of most Washington lobbyists. Rather than crafting the legislative details, they pronounce more sweeping principles and more broadscale criticisms of the Washington establishment as a whole. Indeed, it would be anathema for religious lobbyists to engage in insider transactions with government officials who behave contrary to the moral imperative of religious faith. In most cases, they simply do not desire the kind of clubby relationship that other lobbyists seek. With an orientation toward prophetic condemnation, religious lobbyists remain detached from the insider dealings of Washington politics. Instead they seek to expand[8] the "scope and bias" of the political process[9] by attracting new participants.

To demonstrate their reliance on an outsider strategy, I asked religious lobbyists if they spent more energy on "detailed legislative work" or "involving the public and their members in more general policy trends." All but two groups said their fundamental orientation was directed toward the latter. A slim minority of religious lobbyists get involved in formulating legislation, but the major thrust of even their effort is in education and the mobilization of their grassroots constituency. Most religious lobbyists work to generate new pressure on government officials. They avoid the details of legislation.

In addition, I asked religious leaders specifically if they spent more of their energy on formulating policy or on changing the agenda of Washington. Although agenda setting can be done inside the beltway, it is often an outsider tactic. Most outsiders—including religious lobbyists—are deeply disappointed with the agenda of government. They feel the priorities of government are misguided. They avoid working on the details of existing legislation in favor of transforming the legislative agenda. In my interviews, twenty-one of twenty-eight religious lobbyists said that they focused more energy on influencing the political agenda. Two said their energies were equally divided. The remaining five said that their efforts were more reactive; that the government set the agenda and they responded to it.

Comparing the behavior of religious and nonreligious lobbyists provides the clearest evidence of the unique strategy of religious lobbyists. The comparison should reveal religious lobbyists' greater reliance on outsider tactics.[10] Table 11 shows tactics used at any time by lobbyists. For religious lobbyists, four of the five most commonly used tactics are outsider tactics. More than anything else, religious lobbyists "entered into coalitions with other organizations," "talked with people from the press and the media," "inspired letter-writing or telegram campaigns," and "sent letters to members of their organization to inform them about the organization's activities." None of these tactics involves contacting government officials directly; they are all outsider tactics. In contrast, "contacting official directly" was the only insider tactic used by most religious lobbyists.

Illustrating their contrasting strategy more fully, religious groups differed with other lobbyists most greatly in their use of two tactics: "engaging in protests and demonstrations" and "serving on advisory commissions and boards." Protest politics is the purest form of outsider politics; serving on boards is the archetypal insider strategy. Table 11 shows that 72 percent of religious lobbyists practice protest politics compared to only 20 percent of nonreligious lobbyists. Protestors are literally outside the corridors of power pounding on the doors. A group uses this tactic only when it feels that insider politics is unavailable or will betray the cause. Protestors are seeking to arouse the consciences of the broader public. Among religious lobbyists, the most frequent form of protest is the demonstration on the Capitol steps. As an example, liberal lobbyists gathered countless times during the 1980s at the foot of the Capitol to protest the Reagan policy of aid to the Nicaraguan Contras. In contrast, religious conservatives concentrated their protests on school prayer and abortion. They often gathered outside both the Capitol and the Supreme Court. No tactic is more dissimilar to the cozy clubbiness of the insider game.

In contrast to protests, serving on advisory commissions and boards does not incite more people to participate in the political process. Instead, it is a prototypical insider tactic. It literally involves walking the inner corridors and sitting on official seats in the policy process. In 1982 there were 875 advisory boards and committees in the federal government. These included the Missile Systems Organization Advisory

Group for the Department of Defense and the Health Insurance Benefits Committee for the Department of Health and Human Services. Consistent with their emphasis on outsider tactics, only 34 percent of religious lobbyists serve on advisory boards, while among all lobbyists, twice as many, 76 percent, participate in this activity.

Serving on these boards is fraught with many dilemmas. Some argue that the advisory boards are venues for organized interests to control the policy making process for their own interest. Others argue that these boards provide ways for government to control and channel lobbyists and gain valuable information from them. In either case, it is clear that these boards provide an institutionalized forum for the exchange of information and influence. When lobbyists sit on these boards, they have a formalized place on the inside—not the outside—of the policy process.[11]

While different lobbyists use different tactics, the data also show that all lobbyists use most of the tactics at least once.[12] Twenty of the techniques are used by more than half of the lobbyists. When asked to list all tactics used, regardless of the frequency of use, all lobbyists tend to look somewhat alike. Assessing frequently used tactics is more revealing. When religious lobbyists looked at the entire list of tactics and chose the three that consumed the largest share of their group's time and resources (Table 12), a different pattern emerged. The tendency toward outsider tactics is more pronounced.

As shown in Table 12, religious lobbyists utilize a more limited array of tactics than nonreligious lobbyists. The difference is striking. At least a portion of the broader community of all Washington lobbyists frequently used twenty-three out of twenty-four tactics. Among religious lobbyists, only nine of the twenty-four tactics were heavily used. In addition, four of the five tactics used most frequently by religious lobbyists were outsider tactics. These included "sending letters to members of your organization

TABLE 11
Percentage of Organizations in Each Category Using Tactics in Any Way

RANK	TACTIC	RELIGIOUS INTERESTS	ALL INTERESTS	OVERALL RANK
1	Entering into coalitions with other organizations	100%	90%	6
2	Talking with people from the press and the media	100	86	8
3	Inspiring letter-writing or telegram campaigns	87	84	11
4	Sending letters to members of your organization to inform them about your activities	97	92	5
5	Contacting government officials directly to present your point of view	94	98	2
6	Shaping the government's agenda by raising new issues and calling attention to previously ignored problems	94	84	12
7	Consulting with government officials to plan legislative strategy	91	85	9
8	Mounting grassroots lobbying efforts	91	80	13
9	Testifying at hearings	91	99	1
10	Presenting research results or other information	91	92	4
11	Helping to draft legislation	88	85	10

12	Having influential constituents contact their congressional representative's office	84	80	14
13	Alerting members of Congress to the effects of a bill on their districts	81	75	17
14	Attempting to shape the implementation of policies	83	89	7
15	Engaging in informal contacts with officials—at conventions, over lunch, and so on	81	95	3
16	Engaging in protests and demonstrations	72	20	24
17	Helping draft regulations, rules, or guidelines	68	78	15
18	Publicizing candidates' voting records	66	44	21
19	Filing suit or otherwise engaging in litigation	66	72	18
20	Engaging in direct mail fund-raising for your organization	50	44	22
21	Attempting to influence appointments to public office	45	53	20
22	Serving on advisory commissions and boards	34	76	16
23	Running advertisements in the media about your position on issues	34	31	23
24	Doing favors for officials who need assistance	26	56	19

TABLE 12
Percentage of Organizations in Each Category Indicating That a Tactic Is Used Frequently

RANK	TACTIC	RELIGIOUS INTERESTS	ALL INTERESTS	OVERALL RANK
1	Sending letters to members of your organization to inform them of your activities	66%	12%	10
2	Entering into coalitions with other organizations	50	20	6
3	Contacting government officials directly	44	36	1
4	Inspiring letter-writing or telegram campaigns	34	10	14
5	Mounting grassroots lobbying efforts	34	26	4
6	Shaping the government's agenda by raising new issues and calling attention to previously ignored problems	19	20	5
7	Talking with people from the press and media	9	10	13
8	Testifying at hearings	6	27	2
9	Engaging in direct mail fund-raising for your organization	3	5	17
10	Helping to draft legislation	3	12	11
11	Consulting with government officials to plan legislative strategy	3	19	7
12	Presenting research results or technical information	3	27	3

13	Filing suit or otherwise engaging in litigation	3	4	19
14	Attempting to shape the implementation of policies	0	17	8
15	Alerting congressional representatives to the effects of a bill on their districts	0	14	9
16	Engaging in informal contacts with officials—at conventions, over lunch, and so on	0	10	12
17	Helping draft regulations, rules, or guidelines	0	7	15
18	Having influential constituents contact their congressional representatives' offices	0	6	17
19	Serving on advisory commissions and boards	0	4	18
20	Running advertisements in the media about your position on issues	0	4	20
21	Publicizing candidates' voting records	0	2	21
22	Doing favors for members who need assistance	0	2	22
23	Engaging in protests or demonstrations	0	1	23
24	Attempting to influence appointments to public office	0	0	24

to inform them of your activities," "entering into coalitions with other organizations," "inspiring letter-writing campaigns," and "mounting grassroots lobbying efforts." None of these is an insider strategy. The only insider tactic used regularly by religious lobbyists was their third most frequently used technique: "contacting government officials directly." In contrast, the top three tactics of nonreligious lobbyists were "contacting government officials directly," "testifying at hearings," and "presenting research results." All of these tactics are insider, not outsider, tactics.

Yet, comparing religious lobbyists to the aggregate average of all lobbyists may obscure important differences in lobbying behavior. Other nonreligious lobbyists may behave similarly to religious lobbyists, especially groups concerned with fundamental values and feel that the political process of Washington is corrupt or biased. Disaggregating the data should reveal the degree of this similarity. In Table 13, religious lobbyists' use of outsider tactics is compared with lobbyists from five other types of organizations. As in Table 11, this table refers to the tactics used at any time by lobbyists; it does not refer to the three most frequently used tactics.

In Table 13, the unique pattern of behavior among religious lobbyists diminishes somewhat. As in Table 11, Table 13 shows that most groups use nearly all the tactics in at least a minimal way. Again, the major difference is in the use of protest politics. It is clear that labor unions and religious lobbyists use this strategy more commonly than any other type of lobbyist.

When respondents were asked to name the tactics used most frequently, a unique pattern emerged again (Table 14). With the partial exception of labor unions, religious lobbyists use outsider tactics more than any other type of lobbyist. Their behavior is distinctive. When they choose how to allocate their time and resources, they choose the outsider tactics of inspiring letter-writing campaigns and mounting

TABLE 13
Percentage of Organizations in Each Category Using Tactics

	RELIGIOUS ORGANIZATIONS	UNIONS	CITIZENS' GROUPS	TRADE ASSOCIATIONS	CORPORATIONS
Entering into coalitions	100	100	92	91	96
Talking with people from the press and media	100	95	96	89	67
Inspiring letter-writing campaigns	97	95	86	97	85
Sending letters to members of your organization	97	85	86	97	95
Shaping the government's agenda by raising new issues	94	85	74	77	79
Mounting grassroots lobbying efforts	91	100	71	80	81
Engaging in protests or demonstrations	72	90	25	0	3
Running advertisements in the media	34	55	33	31	31

TABLE 14
Percentage of Organizations in Each Category Indicating Tactic Is Used Frequently

	RELIGIOUS ORGANIZATIONS	UNIONS	CITIZENS' GROUPS	TRADE ASSOCIATIONS	CORPORATIONS
Sending letters to members of your organization	66	13	9	18	6
Entering into coalitions	50	7	17	24	30
Inspiring letter-writing campaigns	34	20	9	12	2
Mounting grassroots lobbying efforts	34	53	44	18	22
Shaping the government's agenda by raising new issues	19	33	27	24	11
Talking with people from the press and the media	9	0	26	9	4
Engaging in protests or demonstrations	0	7	0	0	0
Running advertisements in the media	0	0	0	0	0

grassroots lobbying efforts. They do not choose insider tactics. In contrast, nonreligious lobbyists spend more of their time contacting government officials directly, presenting research results, and testifying at hearings. Engaging in these tactics requires insider contacts. The data show that religious lobbyists reject this style.

Labor unions and citizenship groups behave somewhat similarly to religious lobbyists. Because many labor unions and citizenship groups join religious lobbyists to express more fundamental criticisms of the Washington establishment, this similarity is not surprising. While citizens' and labor lobbyists do not express their criticisms in religious terms, they do object to the priorities of Washington politics. Ralph Nader is a prime example. Clearly, Nader spends little time at the posh watering holes of the nation's capital. Instead, Nader practices outsider politics. His tactics are aimed to agitate and expose industrial and government corruption as widely as possible. In his first foray into politics, Nader sought to change the way in which the nation regulates auto production and safety. Instead of closed-door meetings with government officials, Nader wrote a best-selling book, *Unsafe at Any Speed*,[13] that roused a slumbering citizenry.

Citizens', labor, and religious lobbyists share a common strategy in part because they represent diffuse constituencies and possess relatively meager financial resources. In terms of financial commitments to political campaigns and issues, religious groups and citizen groups both have meager coffers. Labor unions are sometimes more well endowed, but their strength has eroded in recent decades. Beyond their financial status, all these lobbyists also share a world view that rejects many of the values of insider Washington politics, particularly the predominance of big business. A broader theory of lobbying by resource-poor organizations is possible, but it is beyond the scope of this book.

What can be inferred, however, is that both religious and

nonreligious lobbyists use outsider tactics. However, religious lobbyists utilize them more heavily than insider tactics. Religious lobbyists tend to avoid direct dealings with the state. As a result, religious lobbyists are not a part of the bargaining process in which insider tactics are central. Because of that unwillingness, religious lobbyists instead work to generate outside pressure in order to achieve their vision. Thus far, this legislative success has been modest.

SYMBOLIC STRATEGY

Framing symbols is an important political strategy.[14] Lobbyists can use symbols as an outsider tactic to attract new participants into the political process. Alternatively, symbols can serve as an insider tactic. Using an insider approach, lobbyists will define an issue in narrow technical terms. This type of issue definition often focuses on a quantitative analysis of the costs and benefits of an issue. Scholars have termed this type of symbol a "referential" symbol. These symbols do not expand the potential coalition of support. Instead, referential symbols "reduce the scope of meaning associated with an issue by defining it in specific, concrete, neutral terms."[15]

Alternatively, political activists can utilize an outsider strategy and define an issue in impassioned terms. Broad expansive symbols, which scholars term "condensational" are used. Condensational symbols "expand the scope of meaning, defining an issue in abstract, ambiguous, emotionally charged terms."[16] Terms will be simple, powerful, and meaningful to large numbers of people. Using symbols of this kind, religious lobbyists are catalysts for new grassroots support. Because they attract previously uninvolved citizens,[17] using these symbols is an outsider tactic that is consistent with the overall strategy of religious lobbyists.

The religious right is more adept at utilizing condensational symbols than the religious left. For conservatives, promoting school prayer is defined as a constitutional issue.[18] Anti-abortion efforts are defined as "prolife" efforts. Funding for the Nicaraguan Contras is defined as "aid to the freedom fighters." The extension of gay rights is termed a "threat to the family." Trying to ban certain textbooks in the public schools is defined as supporting parental rights.[19] To vote for tuition tax credits is to do nothing less than to affirm the Bill of Rights' commitment to the free exercise of religion. Defining issues in this way identifies the concerns of religious lobbyists with core American values. All Americans are committed to liberty and the family. If they understand the concerns of religious lobbyists in terms of these widely held values, increasing numbers of citizens will join the cause.[20]

Liberal Protestant and Catholic groups have attempted a similar strategy. Their most prominent symbol is the use of the phrase "peace and justice." In addition, Catholics talk about an agenda reflecting "a preferential option for the poor." By this they mean that policy decisions

> must be judged in light of what they do *for* the poor, what they do *to* the poor, and what they enable the poor to do *for themselves*. The fundamental moral criterion for all economic decisions, policies, and institutions is this: They must be at the service of *all people, especially the poor*.[21]

All these definitions are used to broaden the appeal of an issue. However, most observers conclude that the definitions of issues used by liberal groups are not as powerful or as socially significant as the definitions of issues used by conservative groups. This difference may explain why conservative groups have been more influential than liberal groups in recent years.

The symbolic adeptness of conservative groups is also reflected in the names of groups. Conservative groups have

chosen names like the Moral Majority, the American Coalition of Traditional Values, the Liberty Federation, Concerned Women for America, and the Freedom Council. All
of these titles are "condensational symbols" that define the
groups as potentially relevant to most citizens, not only the
members of a narrow sect or denomination. Few liberal
groups use such potent symbols in their names. Lobbyists
for Catholic and mainline Protestant churches simply bear
the names of their denominations. For example, the Washington office of the Presbyterian Church is called exactly
that. The bishops of the Roman Catholic Church call their
Washington office the United States Catholic Conference.
Immediately the significance is limited primarily to members of that denomination. Ecumenical groups are no better.
There, the names are the National Council of Churches,
InterfaithIMPACT, and NETWORK. None of these names
has a potent mass appeal or is readily understood. A few
groups such as Bread for the World have names with
broader symbolic appeal, but they seem to be the exception
among liberal groups. The potential result is less success in
their outsider strategy of cultivating new grassroots support.

LANGUAGE AS A POLITICAL TACTIC

The use of language also has symbolic implications. To
broaden their support beyond a purely religious constituency, religious lobbyists will supplement their religious
framing of an issue with nonreligious language. Interestingly, conservatives were more emphatic than liberals
about the need to avoid religious language. The spokes-
woman for Concerned Women for America said, "I would
say that we avoid religious language. Certainly we use it in
our newsletter from time to time, but there are basic conservative principles that have a biblical base, but do not re-

quire religious language for their articulation."[22] Similarly, Matthew Smyth of Christian Voice added, "I don't think we [use religious language] because quoting from scripture has an uncertain impact on a broader audience."[23] The most forceful statement came from another conservative lobbyist. Ironically, he provided a religious argument for avoiding explicitly religious language. He stated:

> We don't use religious language because we don't have to. When people live against the biblical values that God has instilled in his creation, there is a natural consequence that is bad for everyone. We don't have to condemn people, we just point out the natural consequences of action that is sinful, though we don't explicitly call it sinful. For example, we have opposed gay rights because the proliferation of the gay lifestyle has led to the AIDS epidemic. We have opposed most of the legislation of the feminist agenda because it leads to the disintegration of the family. Concerning abortion, one reason there is a labor shortage at McDonald's is that so many abortions have taken place since 1973. If those abortions had not taken place, there would be no labor shortage. There are natural consequences to man's sin which are bad for God's creation. Our job is to make those consequences more clear.[24]

In his study of the Christian right, Matthew Moen documents the increasing use of secular language by religious lobbyists. He shows an evolution in strategy from an earlier era when the Christian right used more religious and moralistic language to a later era when they avoided this type of rhetoric. While tending to see this change as evidence of the secularization of the Christian right, Moen also notes that religious leaders may use secular rhetoric as a tactic to attract a broader coalition of support.[25]

To be sure, liberal groups also use nonreligious language. They go out of their way to avoid being offensive or alienating. John Carr of the U.S. Catholic Conference stated: "We use religious language to support our positions, but we try to do it in a way that does not depend on religious belief for its persuasiveness."[26] Other liberal leaders articulated the same extreme care in their use of religious language. They employ it, but if there is any possibility of alienating their listener, they avoid it.

However, one lobbyist of a mainline Protestant organization felt that his colleagues used it too much. This person expressed frustration that most mainline Protestant lobbyists could not resist the usage of religious language. The potential existed to damage effectiveness by restricting the scope of meaning.

> For example in our civil rights work, oftentimes we'll do a "sign-on letter." When I drafted the letter, invariably other leaders would say, "Let's add a little here." Invariably I can tell you what gets added. It's a phrase like "as God's people are created equally." It's religious language that becomes a boilerplate. It only alienates potential supporters from outside the religious community.[27]

Others in the community of mainline Protestants and liberal Catholics said that their use of religious language varied depending on the issue and the audience. The Friends Committee on National Legislation's representative remarked:

> I tend to avoid [religious language] because I think it plays into a desire to try to categorize, to pigeonhole, to associate you with whatever is going on in their minds about how religion affects them positively or negatively—in my experience negatively. So I try to carry as little baggage into a situation like that as possible.[28]

The emerging portrait is a religious lobbyist who is, for the most part, very reluctant to use religious language to articulate a public policy position. Although it may be valuable to politicize the faithful, religious language can be detrimental to efforts to expand the size of a coalition. Because it alienates those who do not cast their policy positions in religious terms, it is not a condensational symbol. Religious lobbyists must work to maintain their base of those who share their faith tradition, but they must also attract new supporters in the effort to challenge the ruling elite.

SELF-PERCEPTIONS OF EFFECTIVENESS

To pursue fundamental change is one thing, but to achieve such change is quite another. It is important to assess the effectiveness of religious lobbyists in their goals of altering the basic priorities of government in the United States. To begin to answer this question, I asked religious lobbyists to compare the strength of their organization with the strength of their opponents. Most felt that they were in a weaker position. Eighty-seven percent said they felt weaker than their adversaries; 8 percent said they felt about the same; and 4 percent said they felt stronger.

Table 15 shows the contrast between religious lobbyists and representatives of other organized interests. Religious lobbyists perceive themselves to be in the weakest position in comparison with their opponents. It is clear that churches view themselves as a kind of David against Goliath; indeed, many of them used that metaphor to assess their relative strength. Though more extreme, their self-perceptions resemble those of lobbyists for unions and, to a lesser extent, citizens' groups. Interestingly, this pattern parallels their similarity in preference for outsider tactics discussed earlier in this chapter. Lobbyists who use outsider tactics more exclusively see themselves as weaker than their opponents.

In assessing their relatively weak position, virtually all the leaders who claimed that they were weaker than their adversaries also claimed great power. Ninety percent said that it depends on the issue. On certain occasions, albeit

TABLE 15
Percentage Organization Strength Compared with Opponents

	RELIGIOUS ORGANIZATIONS	UNIONS	CITIZENS' GROUPS	TRADE ASSOCIATIONS	CORPORA- TIONS
Stronger than opponents	4	12	29	22	41
About as strong	8	7	35	41	33
Weaker	87	64	53	18	44

Source: Comparative data from *Organized Interests and American Democracy* by Kay Lehman Schlozman and John T. Tierney. Copyright © 1986 by Kay Lehman Schlozman and John T. Tierney. Reprinted by permission of HarperCollins Publishers, Inc.

only a few, they claimed to be quite effective. Many pointed out that while they were weak in terms of the standards of Washington, they were mighty by another standard. Favoring faithfulness over success leads them to different self-evaluations.

> [Our opponents] have had the jump on us for a while. They've made better use of modern resources and technology and they've been able to amass significant dollars in a short period of time. Generally, though, I think that our strength is much broader and much deeper, but not necessarily as easily excitable, and so if we have more time to get our message out, we do much better.[29]

This reliance upon an alternative measure of effectiveness is related to their expansive goals. Because religious lobbyists seek deeper and more fundamental change, they search for a new measure of success.

> Our agenda, our style, our mission is much different. I measure our performance and our effectiveness on different categories. We ask different questions. We ask how faithful we are to our mission. Are we sharing our teaching with our people effectively, helping people to act on their faith? This task requires different skills, a different style than the National Rifle Association or the Chamber of Commerce. . . . It involves no coercion; it only involves helping people act on their own convictions on what it takes to build a more just society and a more peaceful world.[30]

This comment reveals the nature of religious lobbying. As stated previously in this chapter, fidelity to their faith is the religious lobbyists' measure of success. This conviction often results in a dearth of concrete legislative victories. The final consequence is that religious lobbyists are often "voices crying in the wilderness." Inside the beltway of Washington, they are a relatively insular group of activists. They do not communicate with the established politicians of

Washington as regularly as their secular counterparts. As a result, their calls for change are rarely heeded. Conservatives have failed to make abortion illegal or to reestablish prayer in the schools, yet they hold staunchly to their stands on these issues. Liberal lobbyists have not significantly redirected the priorities of government to the poor. Still they press on.

Occasionally, religious lobbyists have been successful in changing the shape of legislation. When they are successful, the changes are usually significant. During the civil rights movement, Martin Luther King, Jr., and the movement that he led petitioned Congress to make the most fundamental legislative changes in this century. Two decades later church lobbyists' incessant clamoring against the Reagan administration policy of aiding the Nicaraguan contras was partly successfully in slowing the flow of funds. On the eve of one vote, Langhorne Motley, then assistant secretary of state for inter-American affairs, stated, "Taking on the churches is really tough. . . . They are really formidable."[31] Similarly, Cokie Roberts, an ABC news commentator, commenting on the MacNeil/Lehrer NewsHour after one of the House votes on Contra aid, said, "The church groups were the strongest lobby against the package."[32] While many conservative religious groups contended that Contra aid was essential to fight the "Godless Sandinistas," liberal leaders countered by saying that the struggle for peace and justice demanded a different tack. Some went as far as directly supporting the Sandinistas; others simply said that the Sandinistas must not be opposed. In either case, the liberal lobbies won many crucial victories during the 1980s, and the flow of aid to the contras was never steady.

In that same period, the relentless movement against abortion has at least made access to abortion more difficult. While most citizens resist the religious right's desire to criminalize abortion, they also resist the feminist definition of access to abortion as an unmitigated right. The preservation of the ambiguous moral status of abortion may be due in part to the continuing vigilant efforts against abortion by religious groups. In government, Congress's failure to provide publicly funded abortions for poor women and defeat parental notification laws may have stemmed from the work of conservative religious lobbyists.

In conclusion, the data present a distinct pattern for religious lobbyists. Their strategy follows an orientation toward outsider, rather than insider, lobbying tactics. This strategy was expected because insider tactics often involve the necessity of compromise and negotiation. Because religious lobbyists resist compromise, their energy is spent not on bargaining with established players, but on mobilizing the grassroots. They achieve this purpose through traditional communications with grassroots members and through the use of expansive symbols. The overriding goal is to expand the size of their nonelite coalition so that new pressure reflecting religious values can be brought to bear on the policy process. The end result is straddled between a marginalized position in Washington politics and the achievement of significant change—and nothing in between. They want it no other way.

7
CHAPTER

Prophetic Leaders and Their Members

Members of religious organizations do not always agree with the prophetic positions of their lobbyists. As a result, many critics charge religious lobbyists with being "out of step with their members." The charge is often made of mainline Protestants; however, fundamentalist Protestant leaders sometimes take positions on issues without member support.[1] Among Catholics, lay members also disagree with their bishops and other leaders on certain issues. In many instances, religious leaders take positions that are more extreme than their members and justify their action with a theological rationale. Their religious faith requires them to do certain things—regardless of member opinion.

Politicians sometimes discount religious lobbyists because they lack member support. With neither grassroots support from the outside nor campaign contributions from the inside, religious lobbyists' influence in Washington is diminished. In addition to reducing their political power, dissonance between leaders and members threatens the very survival of organizations. Members might leave the organization because of their disagreements with lobbyists who represent them. Religious leaders are then faced with a delicate balancing act. As prophets, they must remain loyal to the radical demands of faith. However, the continuation of their prophetic ministry depends on the continuing existence of their organization. As they utter their prophetic condemnations, they must also keep the peace among their organization's members.

To accomplish this balancing act, religious lobbyists use a mixture of oligarchical and responsive leadership. Using the theory developed in Chapter 3, this chapter will specify the situations that lead to different forms of leadership.

EVIDENCE OF OLIGARCHY

Every religious lobbyist interviewed agreed with the statement that "there are times when lobbyists must go against the views of their organization's members." Other studies have also shown evidence of disagreement between leaders and members of religious organizations. The charge of oligarchy was first leveled in the 1960s concerning mainline Protestants' positions on civil rights and the Vietnam War. Many church leaders issued statements and lobbied the administration without significant member support. The National Council of Churches, Union of American Hebrew Congregations, Methodist Church, United Presbyterian Church in the USA, United Church of Christ, Church of the Brethren, Unitarian Universalists, and World Council of Churches all provided stark and early statements opposing the war.[2] They boldly proclaimed an antiwar position at a time when the war was very popular. Because chuch leaders issued these statements without member support, James Luther Adams concluded that religious lobbyists were "generals without armies."[3]

Looking at different data, A. James Reichley describes this relationship among mainline Protestants as "liberal establishments, moderate laity." Using a 1980 poll of Methodist leaders and members, he shows that on issue after issue, the national staff who did most of the lobbying were consistently to the left of laypersons. For example, only 31 percent of laypersons favored a guaranteed annual income, but 64 percent of the national staff favored such a position. Seventy-five percent of laypersons favored school prayer, in contrast to 29 percent of the national staff. Forty-six percent of laypersons opposed capital punishment, while 79 percent of the national staff opposed it. Reichley also pointed out that strong majorities of Episcopalians, Lutherans, Methodists, Presbyterians, and members of the United Church of Christ voted for Ronald Reagan in both 1980 and 1984, when the public policy positions of the churches' lobbying offices were often more liberal than the Democratic party platform![4]

In the early 1980s, Anne Motley Hallum told of a Presbyterian document that urged citizens to oppose Reagan administration defense policy. Among the suggested actions were the withholding of war taxes, quitting jobs in nuclear weapons industries, noncooperation with the military including disassociation with ROTC programs and military chaplains, and acts of civil disobedience. The church leaders who authored the document advocated these actions in a denomination in which exit polls showed that 68 percent voted for Ronald Reagan.[5]

Beyond the world of mainline Protestantism, divisions in other religious communities abound. Steve Bruce writes about the rise and fall of the Christian right and argues that fundamentalism lost power in part because of internal schisms. In particular, many members were not supportive of Jerry Falwell's involvement in foreign policy issues. Among Roman Catholics, Mary Hanna[6] points to increasing member diversity, and Frank Sorauf notes that the U.S. Catholic Conference does not indisputably represent all Catholics. Some Catholics look to other leaders including local priests and dioceses, state conferences, fraternal groups such as the Knights of Columbus,[7] or political groups such as NETWORK and Catholics for a Free Choice.

Religious leaders are not the only generals without armies; similar charges have been directed at other Wash-

ington representatives. For example, labor unions and professional associations have the same dilemma. Many workers disagree with the political positions of the union leaders
who represent them. On issues of civil rights and foreign
policy, workers have often disagreed with the positions of
union leaders who represent them in Washington. In professional associations, many join with no thoughts of politics. They join to get the professional services provided by
organizations and may not support the lobbying of association leaders.

Like these other group leaders, religious leaders can respond to this situation in a number of ways. They can ac-
quiesce to the views of members and cease lobbying on issues of disagreement or they can lobby despite contrary
member opinion. Consequences follow for ignoring or defying member opinion. The primary fear of many religious
leaders is that opposing member opinion may lead to organizational decline. In mainline Protestant churches, membership has declined, and many point to the prophetic politics of church leaders as the culprit.[8] Though it is difficult to
prove that prophetic lobbying *causes* membership decline,
the loss of members may cause religious lobbyists to feel
insecure. For example, the National Council of Churches,
an organization that includes mainline Protestant denominations, experienced severe staff reductions and budget
cuts during the late 1980s. Many argue that the council's
liberal position on social issues led to its decline.[9]

A MORE COMPLEX PICTURE? EVIDENCE OF
SENSITIVITY TO MEMBERS

In contrast to the indications of oligarchy, much evidence
points to sensitivity to member opinion. During the Vietnam War, while leaders of many religious organizations
rushed forward with their prophetic criticisms of U.S. policy, leaders of other churches waited until public opinion

shifted before issuing statements in opposition to the war. These included the Lutheran Church in America, the American Lutheran Church, the American Baptist Church, the Episcopalian Church, and the Roman Catholic Church. Leaders of these churches acted more consistently with their members' opinions.

Allen Hertzke has argued that the actual "texture" of religious opinion reveals a more complex relationship between leaders and members than such simplistic charges as "generals without an army." Through the enterprising use of national poll data, he found that sometimes there was broad member sentiment for policies advocated by group leaders; sometimes of course there was not. This inconsistent relationship between leaders and members occurred in conservative and liberal lobbies alike, though disagreement was more common among mainline Protestant groups. Using data from the 1984 American National Election Study, Hertzke stated that on the issues of school prayer and abortion, the mainline lobbies indeed fail to represent their members' opinions.[10] On those issues, the majority favors greater restrictions on a women's right to choose an abortion and supports some type of school prayer, positions that are in direct opposition to the clearly stated prochoice and anti-school-prayer positions of church leaders. However, on other issues, such as aid to the Nicaraguan Contras, member opinion is consistent with the forthright anti-contra aid position of mainline church leaders. On all issues, Hertzke found that the Roman Catholic Church seems most representative of its members with its prolife position on abortion and anti-contra-aid position.[11]

Using poll data and the positions of leaders, Hertzke only provided a static snapshot of leader-member relationships. This chapter builds upon Hertzke's important work and develops a more detailed explanation for the shifting and dynamic internal politics of organized religious interests. The relationship between leaders and members will be

analyzed using the tradition of exchange theory. The purpose is to explain the varying relationship between group
leaders and members. Why is there a great disparity between the views of leaders and members on some issues,
but agreement on others?

EXPLAINING THE RELATIONSHIP

Consistent with the tradition of exchange theory, we will
assume that religious lobbyists are rational actors who seek
to maximize a number of goals. They seek both to maintain
their organizations and to remain faithful to their beliefs.
Sometimes these two goals are in conflict. To deal with this
dilemma, religious leaders will accumulate institutional
"profits" that can be used to "buy" or maintain member
loyalty even though members disagree with the lobbying
activity of their leaders. Profits accrue when an organization develops loyalty by providing members with opportunities to grow spiritually and also to meet new people.
Profits also are added when leaders lobby on issues that
members support.[12] In both cases, exchange theorists understand that leaders seek to increase discretion to lobby on
issues that members do not support. Loyalty forged
through other ways may lead members to overlook the dis-
sonant lobbying of leaders. However, the institutional
profits are not infinite. To maintain the organization, a certain amount of responsiveness to members is necessary.
    Building on these theoretical assumptions, the hypothesis
of this chapter is that religious lobbyists will risk their
members' disapproval only on issues that are not salient.
On highly salient issues on which members disagree, they
will usually resist lobbying for fear that their profits are in-
sufficient to buy continuing member loyalty. They may do
some lobbying, but they will not make these issues a high
priority. Occasionally, they may throw caution to the winds

and boldly advocate positions in a highly public way despite member disapproval. However, the cost of such action is high, and lobbyists tend to avoid it.

Data

The hypothesis will be tested on eight issues of the 100th Congress (1987–88) in which religious lobbies were active. These issues were school prayer, abortion, Contra aid, sanctions against South Africa, defense spending, civil rights, welfare reform, and aid to the poor in general. Though other issues could also have been chosen, those eight issues represent the bulk of religious involvement. To test the hypothesis put forward in the preceding section, it is necessary to create a measure of member opinion and issue salience.

To measure member opinion, data from the 1988 American National Election Study were used.[13] The study divides the sample by religious affiliation and asks questions on a broad range of public policy issues. There are some difficulties with the use of these data. First, one can question whether the study measures the opinion of the relevant members. The data show opinion of all members of a religious organization, whether they are active or not.[14] When an organization lobbies, it surely does not look to mass measures of opinion. Instead, leaders will undoubtedly look at subgroups of the broader membership who are most attentive to the action of leaders. Second, the American National Election Study only measures member opinion on public policy issues. It does not measure a member's support for lobbying activity by church leaders on these issues. Since many members may agree with church positions on issues but disagree with the very idea of church lobbying, the data may overestimate member support. Despite these shortcomings, the data give a baseline measure of member support and provide a test of the relationship between leaders and members in religious organizations.

From the American National Election Study data, the congruence of leader and member opinion is assessed. The data measure member opinion by using survey questions and categories that do not exactly correspond with the stated positions of religious organizations. Approximate judgments are made to appraise congruence between leaders and members. For example, general mainline Protestant opposition to school prayer is deemed incongruent with member opinion because a majority of survey respondents support both spoken and silent school prayer. In the tables in this chapter, inferences are summarized by simply noting either congruence or lack of congruence.

Creating a measure of salience is a more vexing task because salience varies a great deal among individuals and groups. To measure societal salience, the number of articles on a given issue in the *Reader's Guide to Periodical Literature* was counted. Since the *Reader's Guide* is the major index of popular media, it is reasonable to assume that a preponderance of articles indicates that an issue is prominent. Certainly, some popular media cover unpopular or obscure issues. But the need to maintain high-level circulations leads to an effort to focus on issues that are salient to readers.

Between 1987 and 1988, there were more than a hundred articles on South Africa, U.S. policy toward Nicaragua, defense, and abortion. On welfare reform, there were twenty-seven articles. On school prayer and civil rights there were fewer than five. In 1984, when school prayer was on the congressional agenda, there were twenty-nine articles. Based upon these disparities, sanctions against South Africa, Contra aid, defense, and abortion are classified as highly salient issues. Welfare reform, school prayer, and civil rights are deemed to be issues of low salience.

MAINLINE PROTESTANTS

Interviews revealed that mainline Protestants had a consensus regarding their priorities in the 100th Congress.

Their high-priority issues were[15] contra aid (against), South Africa sanctions (for), the Civil Rights Restoration Act (for), welfare reform (against the Moynihan bill), and the broader effort to resist cuts in spending for the poor. Abortion (generally prochoice), school prayer (against), Star Wars (against), and the broader issues of defense spending were not priority issues for this group of Protestants in 1987 and '88.[16]

Table 16 shows the relationship between leaders and members on the selected public policy issues. The data show that most mainline Protestant organizations do not enjoy member support on the following three issues: defense, school prayer, and welfare reform. On abortion, the relationship is unclear. On the four remaining issues, there is a fair amount of congruence between the opinion of members and the behavior of organizational lobbyists.

Based upon these data, mainline Protestants are representing their constituents on the issues of contra aid, civil rights, and aid to the poor. On abortion and sanctions against South Africa, the relationship is unclear. They are going against member sentiment on welfare reform, school prayer, and defense. *None* of these issues on which there is clear incongruence between leaders and members is a high-priority issue. This observation confirms my hypothesis. Mainline Protestant lobbyists are risking their members' disapproval only on the low-salience issues of welfare reform and school prayer. Defense policy, a highly salient issue on which there is disagreement with member opinion, was not a high-priority issue during the 100th Congress.[17]

On low-salience issues the risks of oligarchy are low. On high-salience issues, leaders avoid disagreement with members because the costs of oligarchy are too high. Lobbying on these hot issues can ignite members to challenge lobbyists or even leave the organization. On low-salience issues, members will remain loyal despite their disagreement. Church lobbyists work on issues on which members disagree only if the potential for intense member involvement

TABLE 16
Lobby Policy and Lay Member Support by Religious Lobby and Issue

	PRESBYTERIAN	LUTHERAN	EPISCOPAL	METHODIST	AMERICAN BAPTIST
School prayer	–	–	–	–	–
Abortion	–	?	–	–	?
Contra aid	+	+	+	+	+
South Africa santions	+	–	–	–	+
Government aid to poor	+	+	+	+	+
Welfare reform (Moynihan bill)	–	–	?	–	?
Civil rights restoration	+	+	+	+	+
Defense spending	–	?	–	–	–

Note: Lobby policy is determined by specific strategic actions. Member support is determined by denominational sentiment expressed in the 1988 American National Election Study. For welfare reform, data are from 1986 Gallup polls (*The Gallup Report*, nos. 244–45 (January–February 1986): 20; *The Gallup Report*, no. 254 (November 1986): 19). These polls show strong majorities of Protestants favoring workfare requirements in welfare reform (69% for, 24% against, 7% undecided). Given these margins, it seems safe to conclude that mainline Protestants would support the Moynihan welfare reform bill which included workfare requirements.

Key: + Apparent member support for lobby policy
    – Apparent lack of member support for lobby policy
    ? Unclear lobby position or ambiguous lay sentiment

	High salience	Low salience
Leader-member agreement	Contra aid (HP)	Increased aid to poor (HP) Civil rights restoration (HP)
Ambiguous relationship	South Africa sanctions (HP) Abortion (LP)	
Leader-member disagreement	Defense (LP)	School prayer (LP) Welfare reform (HP)

Key: HP = high priority
LP = low priority

FIGURE 3   Mainline Protestant Lobbying

is not present. Figure 3 relates issue salience and leader-member disagreement.

What emerges from this analysis is a portrait of a religious lobbyist who may be sensitive to member opinion but is also driven by a number of other goals. These goals include faithfulness to the tradition of faith and theology, political efficacy, and organizational survival. It is the combination of these motives that prevents the creation of an organization that is either completely oligarchical or completely participatory. If the lobbyist's sole motive were the purity of the cause, then member opinion and organizational democracy would be completely irrelevant. Oligarchy would be the likely result. If on the other hand, the lobbyist's motives focused only on political efficacy and survival, then there would be complete congruence with the views of members. But, with this mix of motivations, the resulting picture is an organization that is far from autocratic but not perfectly participatory. Including the crucial factors of issue salience and organizational priority reveals how leaders attempt to meet all their goals and in the process create an organization that is *roughly* representative. The picture of the church lobbyist as a crusading oligarch, a "general without an army," is refuted by this analysis of mainline Protestants. The actual relationship is more complex and much richer.

FUNDAMENTALIST LOBBYING

In contrast to analyses of mainline Protestants, recent studies of the new right[18] have slighted internal schisms. The Christian right is portrayed as a monolithic organization engaged in political action on a few issues on which there is much consensus. In my interviews, leaders of Christian right organizations also revealed a perception that they were leading a unified movement. The leaders of Christian Voice, the Moral Majority, the Family Research Council, and Concerned Women for America all stated that they could not recall major disagreements within their membership.

A major reason for this congruence is that most of the new right organizations are membership organizations, not the lobbying arms of large denominations. In mainline Protestant denominations, people who join churches are usually oblivious to the lobbying efforts of church leaders. In contrast, people join Christian right organizations solely to seek policy change. Most members of national Christian right organizations are also members of local churches. Most of those churches do not lobby directly, but interested church members supplement their membership by joining a national Christian right organization. They do not join the national organizations to gain fellowship or personal spiritual growth, but only to support political causes. Often their only relationship to the national body is the payment of their annual membership dues through the mail. Because of the shallowness of their membership, they are less likely to remain loyal to an organization if they disagree with the political action of leaders. They may also refrain from voicing disagreement with leaders because they can more easily join other organizations with political agendas in congruence with their beliefs.

Nonetheless, internal disagreement does exist in organizations of the Christian right. Leaders respond strategically to this disagreement. Figure 4 shows that the leaders' position on abortion (prolife), welfare reform (for workfare requirements), defense spending (maintain or increase), and school prayer (support) is consistent with the views of members.[19] Religious lobbying on these issues is representa-

	High salience	Low salience
Leader-member agreement	Abortion (HP) Defense (LP)	Welfare reform (LP) School prayer (HP)
Leader-member disagreement	Contra aid (LP) South Africa sanctions (LP)	Aid to poor (LP) Civil rights (LP)

Key: HP = high priority
     LP = low priority

Note: Leader-member agreement is determined by comparing the policy positions of religious lobbies with measures of member opinion recorded in the 1988 American National Election Study and a 1986 Gallup poll. (The Gallup Report, 1986, Nos. 244–45, 254).

FIGURE 4   Fundamentalist Lobbying

tive of member sentiments. However, on the issues of contra aid, South African sanctions, government aid to the
poor, and civil rights, disagreement exists between leaders
and members. On these issues the leaders supported Contra aid, opposed South African sanctions, opposed government aid to the poor, and opposed the extension of the
Civil Rights Act. Here lobbying by the Christian right is not
representative of the sentiment of church members, and the
Christian right appears oligarchical.

However, when issue salience and lobbying priorities are
added to the equation, my hypothesis is confirmed again.
Fundamentalist Protestants and mainline Protestants relate
to their members similarly. Consistent with my theory, the
leaders disagreed with members only on issues that were
either not salient or of low priority. On the high-priority
issues of school prayer and abortion, there was much member support (see Figure 4). Although fundamentalist leaders
did lobby in opposition to member opinion on South African sanctions, contra aid, civil rights, and aid to the poor,
these were low-priority issues for them. When the issues
are examined more closely, the common picture of an intensely unified Christian right disappears. But Christian
right leaders are responsive to their members, nonetheless.
Strikingly similar to mainline Protestants, fundamentalist
lobbyists have avoided highly salient issues on which there
is leader-member disagreement. Their boldest lobbying has
come on the issues for which they have the most member
support.

The data challenge an interpretation of religious lobbying
that contrasts fundamentalist groups whose leaders have
strong member support with mainline Protestant organizations whose leaders are "out of step" with their members.
In both types of organized religious interests, lobbyists take
issue positions that clash with member opinion. But in neither case does that disagreement occur on highly salient issues. Both fundamentalist and mainline Protestant leaders

work to avoid, intentionally or not, raising the critical ire of their members.

ROMAN CATHOLIC LOBBYING

More than any other church, the Roman Catholic Church is associated with oligarchical decision making. Indeed the church structure includes few elements of organizational democracy in which members might participate. More than other churches, the ecclesiastical structure of Roman Catholicism stresses decision making led from "on high." After Vatican II in the early 1960s, that structure changed somewhat. Now, there is increasing room for lay participation. However, the recent actions by certain Catholic bishops to censure politicians for their positions on abortion show that the church has not become a completely participatory democracy.[20]

In Washington, there are a number of lobbying organizations associated with the Catholic Church. The three main Catholic lobbies are the U.S. Catholic Conference, Catholic Charities, and NETWORK. Each of these three organizations has different priorities, but there are no significant disagreements between them. The U.S. Catholic Conference favors a constitutional amendment banning abortion; NETWORK and Catholic Charities do not lobby on this issue.[21] All three groups favor increased government efforts to help the poor. Catholic Charities is involved primarily in legislation that affects the delivery of social services by nonprofit organizations. On foreign policy, both NETWORK and the U.S. Catholic Conference generally have opposed interventionist policies around the world and supported efforts to reduce the military budget. In sum, there are different emphases among these Catholic organizations, but there are few contradicting positions. The result is a relatively unified effort.[22]

On most issues, there is general consensus between leaders and members. Catholic support for a constitutional amendment banning abortion, against increases in military spending and interventionist foreign policies, and for government efforts to help the poor are generally supported by the members of the Catholic Church. Not surprisingly, abortion is the issue in which the Catholic church has the shakiest support. According to a recent Gallup poll, 46 percent of American Catholics support a constitutional amendment to ban abortion, while 44 percent, almost an equal number, oppose it.[23] The American National Election Study showed that only 16 percent of Catholics favored making abortion illegal under all circumstances, 32 percent would permit it under some circumstances, 20 percent see other conditions in which it might be legal, and fully 32 percent of Catholics favor making it a woman's choice.

Contrary to the expectations of my theory, Catholic leaders have advocated an extreme antiabortion position. Their determined lobbying in favor of a constitutional amendment to ban abortion starkly contrasts with the ambivalent sentiments of lay Catholics. On this highly salient issue, Catholic lobbying is oligarchical, but it is an exception. As shown in Figure 5, Catholic leaders offend public opinion on no other salient issue.

Defying member opinion, the U.S. Catholic Conference aggressively advanced its antiabortion position. It hired a public relations firm to transform public opinion and censured Catholic organizations and public officials who did not share the bishops' position. Despite strong currents of prochoice sentiment among members, Catholic leaders have refused to back down. Instead of yielding to member opinion, they sought to convert it. On this highly salient issue, there were risks to this action. Nonetheless, the Catholic bishops were convinced that the Catholic tradition of moral theology demanded a bold position; there was no room for compromise.

	High salience	Low salience
Leader-member agreement	Contra aid (HP) South Africa sanctions (HP)	Increased aid to poor (HP) Civil rights restoration (HP)
Leader-member disagreement	Antiabortion (HP) Defense (LP)	School prayer (LP)

Key: HP = high priority
       LP = low priority

Note: Leader-member agreement is determined by comparing the policy positions of religious lobbies with member sentiment expressed in the 1988 American National Election Study and a 1986 Gallup poll. (*The Gallup Report*, 1986, Nos. 244–45, 254).

FIGURE 5   Catholic Lobbying

Diminishing Catholic Oligarchy on Other Issues

For the U.S. Catholic Conference, oligarchy is justified because its purpose is to represent just the Catholic bishops, not all Catholics. The policy positions of the U.S. Catholic Conference are determined by vote at the biannual meeting of the 110 U.S. Catholic bishops. Nevertheless, the Bishops are responsive to their members. John Carr, a lobbyist or advocate of the organization, stated:

> That is not to say that ordinary Catholics don't have roles. The peace pastoral and the economic pastoral letters were formed though massive consultation—diocese by diocese. I used to work in the archdiocese in Washington. We had hundreds of parish meetings on the peace pastoral. That all gets fed back to the bishops, who then take it to the national level.[24]

The debate on the letter on economic policy produced three drafts before culminating in a final statement entitled *Economic Justice for All.*[25] The process of drafting that letter was similar to the process used for the bishops' 1982 letter on peace in the nuclear age.[26] The process is unique because, in drafting both letters, the bishops attempted to have a broad-based consultation with people involved on all sides of the issue. A diverse "audience" was assembled, and study and discussion of the drafts were encouraged. Comments were invited. For the economic pastoral letter, the response was so intense that the bishops lengthened the process for completing the final draft by one year.[27]

This consultative process was quite different from the drafting of most previous documents by the American Catholic bishops. Rather than something written from "on high," the letter was a teaching document in which the general public was invited to participate. The content of the letter changed significantly in the drafting process. The final letter encouraged both private individuals and government to do more to help the poor. Recommended government action included provisions for guaranteed health care, employment, and a national minimum (federally funded) income for all. In the drafting process, some specific policy goals were omitted in favor of some more general policy recommendations. But the direction of the recommendations remained clear in all the drafts.

In sum, Catholic lobbying is fairly representative of member sentiment. Only on abortion is support shaky. But on most other issues, the percentage of support approaches two-thirds.[28] As with mainline Protestants, the stereotypical picture of Catholic leaders who are insensitive to member opinion is false. Indeed, the data suggest that there is more member support of Catholic leaders than the representatives of either fundamentalist or mainline Protestants. Since Protestant church structures include less hierarchy and a greater emphasis on the autonomy of individual leaders and parishes, this conclusion is unexpected and ironic. Perhaps Protestant leaders view themselves as autonomous individuals and not part of a large organization.

JEWISH LOBBYING: A PICTURE OF CONSENSUS

Among Jewish groups, there is much consensus among leaders and members. The lobbying priorities of Jewish organizations are (1) aid to Israel, (2) issues relating to the separation of church and state (e.g., school prayer), and (3) civil liberties and economic justice (civil rights and government aid to the poor). Poll data show that their positions on these issues are supported by vast majorities of Jewish citizens. These general priorities have translated into lobbying activity on the following issues: school prayer (against), civil rights (for), abortion (prochoice), day care (for), hate crimes documentation (for), and refugee issues (for greater concern). However, consensus does not mean unanimity. Many American Jews oppose the militancy of Israeli policy toward the Palestinians. Others oppose the expansion of the welfare state. Still others have formed an alliance with Christian right groups over the shared belief that Israel is the promised land of God. However, these positions seem to be those of a distinct minority. No major Jewish lobbying organization espousing these dissenting positions has emerged in America.

Poll data support this assertion of consensus.[29] Strong majorities of Jewish citizens support the positions of the lobbyists who represent them.

In organizations in which there is internal consensus, my model seems inappropriate. The model presumes disagreement between leaders and members. Furthermore, it presumes that leaders will advocate issues in which members disagree at a cost to them. The cost is the increasing tendency of members either to leave the organization or voice their dissent from within. Among Jewish lobbyists, such a calculus does not seem to exist.

INTERNAL CONTROVERSIES

In contrast to the views of many critics, religious lobbyists are sensitive to the opinions of their members. The data show that religious lobbyists avoid working on highly salient issues when members disagree. They may lobby in disagreement with member opinion on issues of low salience, but not on highly salient issues. They make these choices in order to avoid provoking criticism by members.

As a further test of the hypothesis, the nature of intraorganizational politics is explored. Going beyond the simple comparison between the positions of leaders and members, these questions reveal a richer picture of the politics within religious organizations. If lobbyists intentionally avoid provoking members, the internal political processes should be relatively harmonious. To determine whether these processes are harmonious, I first asked lobbyists to tell me if they could identify internal controversies in their organizations. Then, I asked lobbyists if organizational elections were contested. The results of the interviews provide some challenge and some support to the picture of internal harmony. Religious lobbyists pointed to frequent internal conflicts on specific issues; however, they admitted few instances of contested elections. The conflicts within religious organizations usually have not translated into opposing organized factions that work to elect new officers and board members.

Concerning internal conflicts, 53 percent of the groups—more than half—reported a controversial issue in their organization. Some, like Mark Pelavin of the American Jewish Congress, viewed controversies as an inevitable part of organizational life. He said, "There are controversies all the

time. That's what makes the meetings interesting."[30] Glen
Stein of the Union of American Hebrew Congregations
noted that the biggest controversy is "whether or not to establish a Washington office that engages in lobbying." He
said that there is a minority of congregants who believe that
our religious principles should lead us to shun lobbying."[31]

Among the sixteen group leaders who reported controversy in their organization, fourteen were characterized as
denominations, not membership organizations. More members of religious denominations voice their dissent and try
to change denominational positions. Among membership
organizations, simply quitting the organization seems to be
the more prevalent way of expressing dissent. This difference can be explained by the prevalence of members who
join churches with no thought of lobbying denominational
leaders.

In most organizations, controversy seemed to be confined consistently to one or two issues. For the Friends
Committee on National Legislation, these were abortion
and gay rights. For the Mennonites, the issues were abortion and South African sanctions. A lobbyist for the Evangelical Lutheran Church in America pointed to contra aid
and school prayer. For the remaining groups, lobbyists
mentioned a range of issues including child care, agriculture, and economic justice issues in general.

The most frequently mentioned controversial issues were
abortion and gun control. Abortion was mentioned by five
lobbyists; gun control was mentioned by four. These
seemed to be the "hot button issues." Donna MortonStout
of the Presbyterian church reflected on the controversy in
her church over abortion and gun control and noted the
irony that the most meager lobbying produced the greatest
controversy.

> Overall, the biggest controversy in our organization is
> about abortion and gun control, even though we don't
> spend any money on those issues. We are members of the

Religious Coalition for Abortion Rights, and we are
members of the National Coalition to Ban Handguns. But
we do not give any financial support to either one of them.
Among our staff, very little time is spent on those issues.
But in terms of the constituency response, we get the most
flak on those two issues.[32]

Another lobbyist, Mary Jane Patterson of the Presbyterian
Church, described the controversies of her organization by
talking about ideologically extreme groups within her denomination. She stated:

In all the major mainline denominations, there are groups
of people who are ideologically wedded to the far right.
That's the only way I know how to describe it. They say
that we should not be involved in some of the issues on
which we work.[33]

Patterson seemed to welcome this controversy and dissent.
She displayed no inclination toward downplaying the dissent or portraying it as limited to a few issues. Indeed, she
said, "I think this is part of the glory of democracy—to be
living in a republic where people can feel free to say what
they have to say. For me, that's stimulating."[34] The representative of the Episcopal Church made the same point. He
said "the very nature of the deliberative process will lead to
controversies and hopefully resolve them. Indeed, the process is designed to do that."[35]

Though there is controversy in many organized interests,
particularly institutional religious interests, the controversies reported by the lobbyists did not occur on salient issues
or on issues that were a major priority to the organization.
Controversies on abortion and gun control were reported,
but these issues had a low priority among the lobbyists'
agenda items.

Among the remaining groups, whose representatives
could not recall a major controversy, consensus was the
norm. Most groups simply did not work on issues for
which there was a lack of consensus. Coalitions like IM-

PACT and the National Association of Evangelicals, though different from each other in theological and political beliefs, did not lobby on issues on which their member church bodies disagreed. IMPACT avoided the issues of Middle East policy and abortion because the coalition was deeply divided on those issues. The National Association of Evangelicals ignored defense issues because the leaders did not want to offend the historic peace churches in their organization.[36]

Consensus also kept the peace among membership groups, including both liberal and conservative groups. Lobbyists for more liberal groups like Bread for the World and NETWORK both reported that there was "a fair amount of consensus in their organization." Consensus is never complete, but there were no deep controversies in either organization.[37] The one exception among liberal membership organizations was Church Women United. That organization's work on the issue of abortion offended the positions of many Catholic women.[38] Among conservative membership organizations, also, consensus was the norm. None of the conservative lobbyists mentioned any type of controversy in their organization, nor could any recall criticism from their members. This picture of consensus is consistent with other research on the Moral Majority.[39]

The overall picture shows that among institutional religious interests, there is internal controversy on issues that were either of low salience in society or low priority for the organization. This finding is consistent with the larger argument of this chapter. Among membership organizations, consensus is most prevalent. It is exceptional when the positions of leaders are significantly contrary to the views of members.

Organizational Elections

Organizational elections can reveal conflict in an organization. Major conflicts often incite the creation of opposing factions that compete with each other for control. Among religious institutions, the election of officers and boards for the lobbying arms of religious organizations was assessed. My purpose was to determine whether elections were contested and, if so, whether candidates came from competing factions within the organization. According to Schlozman and Tierney, this emphasis on the nature of electoral competition is based on the assumption that stable competing factions enhance the participatory nature of organizational politics. In such organizations and societies, candidates are more likely to take distinguishable positions on issues. The result is higher rates of participation and an increased likelihood that voters understand the choices offered in elections.[40]

Like other organizations, not all religious organizations even have elections. As shown in Table 17, the proportion of religious organizations holding elections is slightly less than the proportion of all organized interests. Seventy-seven percent of religious organizations elected their officers in elections. This proportion is similar to that of citizens' groups that had elections (73 percent), but less than the 100 percent of labor unions that hold elections. Among religious organizations, the groups that did not have elections were membership organizations. Some groups chose their officers from within.

In terms of enduring factions, the results are mixed. It is striking that so few factions, as seen in Table 17, are present among religious organizations. Among the ten groups with contested elections, only one organization included factions that endured through a number of consecutive elections. This organization was the Baptist Joint Committee. In the Southern Baptist Convention, moderates and fundamentalists have waged a fierce battle about theology, politics, and the very control of the church.[41]

Among all the remaining organizations, many have elections, some of which are contested. But the cleavage lines of the organization are changing constantly. Many organizations expressed some surprise at the lack of durable factions. Matthew Ahman of Catholic Charities said, "That's a good question because you would think that after 75 to 80

TABLE 17
Electoral Competition

	RELIGIOUS ORGANIZATIONS	UNIONS	CITIZENS' GROUPS	TRADE ASSOCIATIONS	ALL MEMBERSHIP GROUPS
Officers chosen in elections (%)	77	100	73	85	86
Elections ordinarily contested (%)	50	68	54	31	46
Parties or factions in contested elections (%):					
1. As a proportion of such organizations having contested elections	10	64	43	50	53
2. As a proportion of all such organizations choosing officers in elections	7	37	27	14	23
3. As a proportion of all such organizations	5	37	20	12	20
Number in category (*n*)	20	19	15	34	102

Source: Comparative data from *Organized Interests and American Democracy* by Kay Lehman Schlozman and John T. Tierney. Copyright © 1986 by Kay Lehman Schlozman and John T. Tierney. Reprinted by permission of HarperCollins Publishers, Inc.

years, there ought to be some camps fairly rooted with some strength. But I don't think there are any."[42] Mark Pelavin of the American Jewish Congress stated that competitive elections in his organization were more "personality oriented" rather than related to any enduring issue divisions.[43] Arthur Simon of Bread for the World stated, "It's more random, that's my impression. Occasionally there is a flurry of support for a particular candidate. But it is really quite random."[44] Leland Wilson of the Church of the Brethren notes that elections in his organization are "pretty low-key; most candidates don't wear labels."[45]

The lack of competing factions is additional evidence supporting a general picture of consensual organizations. In many religious organizations there is conflict. Often the conflict is intense. However, the conflicts are episodic and not related to enduring factions that persist over time. In only one case, the Baptist Joint Committee, did internal conflict threaten the direction or survival of the organization. Confirming the larger hypothesis of this chapter, organizational leaders usually avoid offending members, because such actions may threaten the life of their organization. Thus even in organizations where leaders are radically different from their members, they take steps to avoid arousing an organization-threatening controversy. This does not mean that leaders will always follow the exact wishes of members. As this chapter has shown, leaders sometimes take stands without the support of members. But they also demonstrate a responsiveness to member concerns and a commitment to a democratic organizational process.

CONCLUSIONS

This analysis shows that religious organizations are neither completely autocratic nor completely participatory. Instead, the style of internal politics varies and is determined by a variety of factors including both the political context and the goals and motives of leaders. The behavior of religious lobbyists is similar to the behavior of members of Congress and other political actors. Just as members of Congress seek to gain reelection, religious lobbyists desire to maintain their organization. To do that they engage in a specific pattern of behavior.

It is ironic that lobbyists who perceive themselves as prophets should avoid internal controversy and be sensitive to member opinion. But prophets are not solitary critics. They exist in a larger context, an organization that pays their salaries and provides them with an office to serve as a base in Washington. Securing this base requires a certain amount of organizational maintenance and even conflict avoidance. The prophetic action of lobbyists has limits. Transgressing those limits can put the very survival of a lobbyist's Washington operation at risk. Even prophets must eat.

8
CHAPTER

Prophetic Lobbyists and the Future of American Politics

Differing profoundly with their secular counterparts, religious lobbyists boldly speak for the deepest convictions of people of faith. In doing so, they represent a tradition of values that has always been at the heart of American politics and society. Religion's thoroughgoing presence in American politics led one historian to declare the United States "a nation with the soul of a church."[1] Yet because religious faith can demand fierce devotion, religious involvement in politics also strikes fear in those who shudder at religious political activism or deem it illegitimate on American soil. True to this lineage, a politics grounded in religion inspires both inspiration and trepidation.

As a result, the relationship between religion and politics is paradoxical. People fear religious political activism, but they also spontaneously seek it. Fear of religion's involvement in politics is born from memories of religious persecution. Many immigrants came to America to escape the heavy hand of the dominant church in their home country. Native Americans and African-Americans still experience this kind of persecution. This fear of religious dominance translates into the conviction that only the individual—not the state—can determine personal faith. When organized religion lobbies for public polices, some view it as another means of persecution. Advocating religiously rooted public policies becomes offensive or oppressive to those who disagree, whether they are members of other religions or of no religion at all.

Interestingly, although religion divides societies, it can also provide unity and stability. In the United States, conflicts are rarely along religious lines. Despite professing allegiance to a resplendent diversity of religions, most U.S. citizens also share a unifying civil religion that features common values, including a quasi-religious devotion to the state. The central American values of individual liberty and social justice gain much support from religious belief. The commitment to liberty and individual autonomy stems from a theology of *imago dei,* the religious conviction that humans are created in the image of God. Out of this belief comes the conviction that human rights are not up for negotiation; instead they are ordained by God. In addition to liberty, morality and justice are central tenets of religious faith. Religious faith inspires a zeal for justice that leads to efforts to end poverty and restore traditional morality. The zealotry of such efforts sometimes conflicts with the protection of liberty, but religious citizens and organizations often seek to balance both aspects of faith.

Maintaining this balance, all the lobbyists in this study—both liberal and conservative—shared a commitment to religious liberty. None call for curtailing the right of Americans to choose their own faith; few call for any kind of Christian America. These assurances should silence the worries about religious intolerance. Religious activists support religious liberty because it is in their own interests. If one religion dominates the state, other religions will suffer under the new regime. The apprehension of such dominance leads religious lobbyists to support the consensus for religious liberty in the United States.

Nevertheless, instances of religious intolerance and injustice may occur. Some fear the political correctness of the religious left. Others tremble at conservative Christian hostility to civil rights legislation and the equal rights of women. Although such views can be unpalatable to many, those who espouse them fervently believe that important religious and moral values are threatened. To those who disagree, it is important to recall that the U.S. political system guards against the enactment of intolerant public policies. Checks and balances and constitutional guarantees against authoritarian rule make it exceedingly difficult for authoritarian factions—religious or otherwise—to dominate. As a result, deeply principled political activists can be welcomed into the political process because any anti-democratic proposals would not likely survive the give and take of American politics. Politics in the United States does separate the wheat from the chaff of religiously inspired politics.

With some caveats, most Americans welcome religion in their politics. No one has ever won the presidency without declaring some kind of religious belief! Analyzing the 1988 election, Garry Wills argued that a primary cause of Dukakis's defeat was his thoroughly secular world view; he was the first secular candidate for president of the United States.[2] In contrast, Fred Barnes argued that Bill Clinton won the 1992 election in part because he was a "stealth" religious candidate. That is, he did not refer explicitly to his religious faith, but he used religious concepts like the "new covenant" to communicate his policies. Barnes contended that, with 90 percent of the electorate claiming a belief in God, the use of religious imagery helped Clinton win the election.[3]

Since religious convictions often represent people's deepest beliefs, it is not surprising that those beliefs should have political ramifications. Theologian Paul Tillich defined religious faith as one's "ultimate" concern.[4] If a concern is ultimate, it profoundly influences all of one's life—including politics. It is this depth of religious conviction that leads citizens both to fear and to seek religious involvement in politics. People fear the involvement because the power of religious beliefs may lead to intolerance of opposing views. Opposing forces are a challenge to nothing less than one's faith. Yet people seek religious politics because a primary source of moral convictions is religious faith. Without religion, our politics would be less moral. Religion is not the only source of morality, but it constitutes a vital part of the American moral tradition.

Because of the fear of some religiously grounded politics, many resent or oppose religious lobbyists. Some charge that religious lobbyists advocate extreme causes not shared by the members of their organization. More profoundly, they challenge the essence of the religious lobbyist's claim to translate and lobby on behalf of a religious interest. Can one derive viable political claims from a religious interest? To these critics, religious faith is completely separate from politics. Religious lobbying is a fundamental violation of the separation of church and state.

Indeed, the money, persuasion, and bargaining that make up Washington politics do seem distant from the simplicity and purity of religious faith. For this reason, many religious people themselves contend that political involvement can diminish their faith in the ultimate. The broad principles of faith must be distinguished from specific public policies, they add. Religious faith may call believers to love their neighbors, but it is silent on the finer points of particular public policies. Religious faith calls people to bring forth justice but says nothing about the proper position on welfare reform.

But distinctions between general principles of faith and specific policies are made more easily in the abstract than in the particular predicament of politics. The failure to connect religious faith with politics can render faith irrelevant and rob it of its vitality. If faith is ultimate, it will have ramifications for all aspects of life. It should affect one's personal lifestyle choices and one's political commitments. Admitting uncertainty, religious lobbyists then must work with the full knowledge that others, even their own rank and file, may legitimately find different connections between faith and politics. Liberty and tolerance are a part of religious political activism.

Because they are religious, these lobbyists have a peculiar style of lobbying. By Washington standards, they are political misfits. This noncomformity is their greatest weakness—and their greatest strength. It is a weakness because many religious citizens seek political involvement but fear being overwhelmed or dirtied by politics. As a result, most churches and synagogues devote meager resources to Washington representation. A denomination with several million members may employ a small Washington staff. Many religious organizations choose to have a Washington office only to make a symbolic statement. Faith and politics do mix; however, reticence about politics precludes religious lobbyists from realizing their full potential strength.

Compounding the problem of their small numbers, religious lobbyists advocate a broad range of public policies as if they were seeking to usher in the "kingdom of God." Indeed, many use this very language. As a result, a small staff is involved in an astonishing range of issues, often including defense spending, human rights, welfare policy, foreign aid, school prayer . . . and more. The breadth of their involvement precludes the possibility of mastering legislative details. Instead, religious lobbyists spend much of their time articulating broad moral principles; they usually leave the details to others. Because this approach is so foreign to elected officials and secular lobbyists, religious lobbyists are often marginalized in Washington.

Because disillusionment with Washington politics is now at a peak, citizens may increasingly respect political activists who stand at the margins of Washington politics. Unraveling the causes of citizens' disenchantment is complex;

however, a central problem is a perception of lobbyists buying off the public interest with dollars gleaned from the deep purses of special interests. As a result, the broader will of the people is thwarted, and pressing national problems go unaddressed. Responding to this situation, the role of the prophet in American politics is crucial. They remind citizens of their ethical lapses and keep the polity focused on crucial problems. Assuming this role, religious lobbyists serve as a kind of national conscience. Insistently, they provide a moral guide at the margins of the political debate.

In their own way, religious lobbyists work to transform U.S. politics. To them lobbying is more than the search for small changes in legislation. It is more than the mercenary search for the material gain of one's client. Instead, it is about transforming the agenda and content of American politics. It is about infusing politics with a moral concern born from a long religious tradition. To be sure, translating ultimate convictions into choices about different pieces of legislation is a vexing process. Nevertheless, religious lobbying does introduce moral concerns into the political process. These lobbyists remind citizens to take care of the powerless and guard the fragile families of America. In these days when more and more people slip into poverty and increasing numbers of families are unable to stay together, this concern is paramount. Without religious reminders, who will care for the powerless? Who will focus on the family? Surely, many nonreligious people will advocate these causes—but religion's absence will certainly diminish their strength.

In their work, religious lobbyists often formulate policies that are out of the mainstream of American politics. For the most part, they occupy the extreme left and extreme right of the political spectrum in the United States. Perhaps these extreme positions, more than anything else, lead people to dismiss or fear religious lobbying. But there is a value in having a clear articulation of extreme positions. Religious political activism sometimes has a sharper vision.

For example, liberal lobbyists have long criticized U.S. foreign policy for its excessive militarization and fixation with an anticommunist crusade. In making these criticisms, they may have revealed a better estimate of the threat of communism than the foreign policy experts. Perhaps, only perhaps, they could see the weakness of communism long before the collapse of that movement. On the right, conservative lobbyists early on expressed concerns about education and the family. They bemoaned the absence of school prayer and the growing secularization of the classroom. Now all of society is worried about education. The remedies vary greatly, but there is a consensus on the problem—the absence of discipline and values.[5]

It was also religious conservatives who early expressed concern about the breakdown of the family. Now this is a concern of both left and right. Not everyone agrees with the conservative vision of traditional nuclear families, but everyone knows that we must find better ways to support families and their children. Because so many social problems stem from the withering bonds among family members, the problems of the family must be addressed. It was religious conservatives who were among the first to bring public attention to these concerns.

So, religious lobbyists make an important contribution to American politics. Bringing previously quiescent citizens into the process, they make politics more democratic. Challenging elite perspectives, they make politics more participatory. Representing important values, they also serve as an antidote to political debates that sidestep moral significance. Finally, their position on the margins of American politics gives them a distinctive vantage point that can produce illuminating new perspectives on the critical problems that face the United States.

THEORETICAL SIGNIFICANCE

This study is grounded in the tradition of interest group scholarship in the discipline of political science. Primarily, I have turned to the pluralist tradition as a way to explain the political behavior of religious lobbyists. There are many good reasons for this choice. Among them is the extremely pluralistic character of American religion. In the context of a constitutional structure that guarantees religious liberty and prohibits the establishment of a state church, a dizzying variety of religions have emerged. The variety is unmatched in other parts of the world; no other nation contains the wide array of religions that is found in the United States.[6]

In political science, the tradition of analytical pluralism has endured much criticism. Primarily, the critics cite the inability of pluralist thought to explain why some interests organize while others do not. Addressing this weakness, the critics of pluralism have explained much about the logic of group formation. We now know much about why many groups do not form around shared interests. But the critics of pluralism do not tell us much about the tactics that interest groups use to change the formulation of public policy. The critics focus more on explaining elite dominance than on counter-organizing strategies. Because the strategies and tactics of organized interests are the primary topic of this book, I have turned to the tradition of pluralism as a robust analytic framework.

Pluralism begins to clarify the tactics that groups use to influence the policy process. But the pluralist tradition lacks a deeper explanation concerning why groups pursue different strategies. Pluralist theory tells us that groups will generate pressure; however, the concept of pressure is vague. As a result, the pluralist tradition usually functions as a kind of heuristic device, and pluralist studies usually do not tell us more than which groups are applying pressure.

Such studies are valuable in establishing the importance of groups and for describing what groups do. However, they do not contribute to explanations of why groups do what they do.

If all groups did the same things, such explanations would be unnecessary. But groups use a variety of tactics to generate different kinds of political pressure. The absence of explanations of these varying tactics is illustrated most aptly in studies of interest group behavior that focus on developing a list of a broad range of tactics with a frequency distribution of how often each tactic is used.[7] The studies are more descriptive than explanatory.

Though I do not attempt to provide a comprehensive model for explaining the tactics and strategies of the entire interest group system, I have focused on the weaknesses of pluralism in explaining the behavior of a more ideologically extreme universe of organized interests. In political science, few studies have focused on more radical or extreme interest groups. The distinctiveness of radical groups is their rejection of the politics of compromise and incrementalism. For religious groups, a compromise is often interpreted as a breach of faith. Viewed this way, issues are perceived in black-and-white terms; there is no middle ground. As a result, there is a reluctance to engage in the bargaining process that is central to most understandings of pluralist politics. Religious groups, therefore, focus more energy on the generation of grassroots pressure. In the categories used by interest group scholars, religious lobbyists focus more on indirect or outsider, rather than direct or insider, strategies.

The end result is a marginalization of religious lobbyists. In Washington, the more prominent and frequent political strategy is bargaining among groups and incremental rather than radical change. The rejection of these tactics by religious lobbyists can make them political misfits. In the Washington lobbying community, religious lobbyists are often viewed as outside the mainstream. But while this isolation is often viewed as a political weakness, it can also be a strength. It is a strength when religious lobbyists generate enough pressure to make fundamental change a real possibility. The religious right seemed to reach this point in the 1980s. Though ultimately unsuccessful, the religious right influenced the politics of school prayer and abortion. More liberal religious groups seemed to reach this point during the civil rights battles of the 1960s and the struggle over contra aid in the 1980s. In each of these periods, organized religious interests were able to challenge core values of American politics and culture.

Focusing on the refusal to compromise advances the pluralist tradition. The distinction that emerges is between mainstream groups that seek compromise and radical groups that avoid it. The significance of the distinction lies in the connection between political goals and political tactics. Mainstream groups focus primarily on seeking incremental change. This focus results in the use of both insider and outsider tactics. Insider tactics are used to negotiate the compromise. Outsider tactics are used to generate pressure to accomplish the incremental change. Radical groups seek more fundamental or radical change. They are less inclined to use insider strategies because such tactics are usually not helpful in achieving radical change. To achieve widespread change, a greater focus on outsider strategies is necessary.

There are certainly times when radical groups use insider strategies. If great amounts of outside pressure are generated, religious lobbyists can move to greater emphasis on an insider strategy. At that point, the strategy is used more to negotiate the terms of a political triumph than to reach a compromise. As a result, radical groups are either irrelevant or extremely influential. Because the possibility of the triumph of a radical strategy is rare, organized religious interests will use insider tactics more rarely than their secular counterparts. This is a distinction that pluralist theory has not developed.

To be sure, this distinction has its shortcomings. Sometimes religious lobbyists do engage in an insider strategy in order to gain incremental change, as in the debates over charitable tax deductions and equal access legislation.[8] My argument is not that religious groups rely solely on an outsider or indirect strategy. Instead, it is that religious lobbyists emphasize this strategy. This tendency is present because religious lobbyists perceive a tremendous gulf between their values and the values of the Washington establishment. This perceived gulf prevents religious lobbyists from engaging in insider lobbying.

THE FUTURE OF RELIGION IN AMERICAN POLITICS

Organized religion will continue to influence politics in the United States. The crucial question is, To what degree and to what effect? In the future, it is possible that the outsider or prophetic stance of religious lobbyists will result in a continued marginalized status. The lack of media coverage of the religious left is evidence of a marginal role. On the right, the recent curtailment of lobbying by many religious conservatives is evidence of a retreat from involvement in Washington politics.[9]

Although religious conservatives have withdrawn from involvement in Washington politics, they continue to be involved in other arenas of politics. They focus on electoral politics rather than Washington lobbying. Building on their work in the 1994 election, they will continue to influence and even dominate some state political parties. Their presence in the national Republican party is surging. In addition, should Pat Robertson or another religious conservative run for the presidency again, he can be expected to have an enthusiastic following.

On the religious left, it is also possible that the influence of religion will increase. This will occur if vast segments of public opinion come to support the position of religious lobbyists. Perhaps the calls for economic justice by the religious left may strike a respondent chord in the American public in the 1990s. Certainly, the powerful response to Kevin Phillips' analysis of the growing gap between rich and poor might lead one to expect a positive reception to the economic analyses of the religious left.[10] Phillips argues that this growing gap was caused by the policies of the Reagan and Bush administrations, and thus a liberal backlash with religion playing a role could be possible. However, the resounding Republican victories in the 1994 election render this possibility increasingly remote.

Both liberals and conservatives have been ardent advocates of greater justice and liberty. With that perspective, we can expect religious political activists to resist and challenge the unjust and intolerant policies of the state. When they do, religion will make society more inclusive and more democratic. There are many examples of success in such efforts. In working to end slavery and guarantee civil rights, religious political activists made the United States more tolerant of the rights of minorities. Beyond the United States, in places as diverse as Poland and the Philippines, religion has been a significant part of the resistance to totalitarian governments. In each of these cases, religion has worked to challenge the unjust and antidemocratic policies of the state. By remaining in Washington, but not of it, organized religion has provided a critical force for greater liberty and justice in the United States and around the world.

Methodology and Sample

In the discipline of political science, the study of religious interests can be described as data-poor. None of the major surveys of interest group behavior focuses on religious groups as a separate category. There are no data archives on religious interest groups. In addition, the peculiarity of religious involvement in American politics further confounds the collection of data. Most religious lobbyists are not officially registered as lobbyists. Being unregistered preserves the 501(c)3 status of their organization,[1] but it makes it more difficult to collect data about their work. In addition, only a handful of religious organizations have political action committees, thus blocking another data source. Confounding the researcher's task even more, newspaper reporting of the political involvement of religious organizations is erratic,[2] and the internal record keeping of religious organizations is inconsistent.

This poverty of information necessitates the collection of new data. Because no one has collected data specifically about religious interest groups, the only remaining alternative is to enter the arena of the religious lobbyist and seek data from direct contact with the political actors themselves. Accordingly, my primary research method is in-depth interviewing of religious leaders. These interviews are supplemented by a modest amount of quantitative survey data concerning the political behavior of religious leaders and the attributes of religious organizations. I administered the survey at the close of each interview.

While the shortage of data has necessitated my research strategy, the interview is an appropriate research method because I wanted to gain a sense of how leaders of religious lobbying organizations viewed the political process. In attempting to understand the perspectives of these lobbyists, it was necessary to go to their "turf" and let them tell me about their political goals and behavior. Consistent with a qualitative methodology, "the important reality is what people perceive it to be."[3] Toward that end I asked religious lobbyists how they saw the Washington political process and their place in it. I wanted to learn how they viewed the political establishment and process. What goals did they have? What strategies did they use to achieve their goals? How do they relate to their members? How effective are they? What does being effective mean to them? These interviews form the primary data source of this project; I use the data in two ways. First, the data provide a qualitative picture of the world of religious lobbyists. Second, the data are used to test hypotheses about the behavior of religious lobbyists derived from the theories that were developed in Chapter 3.

THE UNIVERSE OF ORGANIZED
RELIGIOUS INTERESTS

During November 1988, June 1989, and January 1994, I interviewed the leaders of thirty-two organizations. They are listed in Table 18. Those organizations formed a diverse "sample" that included Catholic, Protestant, and Jewish groups of varying theological and political beliefs. In addition to this diversity of theological and political views, the

TABLE 18
Organized Religious Interests

U.S. Catholic Conference
NETWORK
Catholic Charities
National Council of Churches
Washington Office of the Episcopal Church
Presbyterian Church USA—Washington Office
United Methodist Church, General Board of Church and Society
Evangelical Lutheran Church in America, Office of
  Governmental Affairs
United Church of Christ, Office for Church and Society
American Baptist Churches USA
American Friends Service Committee
Friends Committee on National Legislation
Mennonite Central Committee
Church of the Brethren, Washington Office
Baptist Joint Committee for Public Affairs
National Assocation of Evangelicals
General Conference of Seventh Day Adventists
Lutheran Church–Missouri Synod
Christian Voice
Concerned Women for America
Family Research Council
Moral Majority
American Jewish Committee
American Jewish Congress
Union of American Hebrew Congregations
Religious Task Force on Central America
Interfaith Action for Economic Justice
IMPACT[a]
Association for Public Justice
Bread for the World
Christic Institute
Unitarian Universalist
Christian Legal Society[b]
National Office of Jesuit Social Ministries[b]
Americans United for the Separation of Church and State[b]

(continued)

TABLE 18 *Continued*

Anti-Defamation League–Washington Office[b]
American Freedom Coalition[b]
Religious Coalition for Abortion Rights[b]
American Israel Public Affairs Committee[b]
Catholics for a Free Choice[b]
Christian Coalition[b]
Christian Life Commission of the Southern Baptist Convention[b]
Church World Service/Lutheran World Relief[b]
AIDS International Interfaith Network[b]
Traditional Values Coalition[b]
Inter-religious Health Care Access Campaign[b]
Churches of Christ, Scientist—Washington Office[b]

[a]Interfaith Action for Economic Justice and IMPACT have merged to form a single organization, Interfaith IMPACT.
[b]Not able to interview.

organizations in this study were diverse in structure. I interviewed representatives of denominations, direct-mail membership groups, and representatives of social service agencies. As discussed in the opening chapter, I refer to my sample of groups as organized religious interests. The diversity of my "sample" enabled me to think broadly about both the unity and diversity of religious lobbyists. While I will try to describe the broad spectrum of the religious lobbying universe, I focus primarily on the unity and similarity of religious lobbyists.

I identified a universe of forty-seven religious interest groups that operated at the national level of American politics and had offices in Washington, D.C. Identifying this list of groups was not without its difficulties. Because none of the large studies of interest groups use separate religious categories, I had to rely on a limited number of previous studies.[4] In addition, I consulted the *Encyclopedia of Associations* and *Washington Representatives*. Because the compilers of *Washington Representatives* had a separate indicator for religious organizations, this volume was quite helpful although some groups listed had only a minimal involvement in Washington lobbying.[5] As stated in Chapter 1, I excluded such groups from this study. Finally, *U.S. Religious Interest Groups: Institutional Profiles*, by Paul J. Weber and W. Landis Jones, is an immensely valuable resource that was published near the end of my project.[6]

In the interviewing process, there was some expansion in the list of religious interests, but this expansion was minimal. My goal was to create a comprehensive list of all religious organizations that are active in national politics. Undoubtedly, I missed some organizations or incorrectly disqualified them from my universe of groups. There is no way to verify this belief except to submit my "sample" to other students of religion and politics and await their additions or subtractions from my list.

THE INTERVIEW PROCESS

Of the forty-seven groups that I identified, I interviewed thirty-two. I did not randomly chose these thirty-two. Rather, I spoke to the thirty-two groups who were, generally speaking, the largest and most prominent. In that sense, I used a rough form of purposive sampling. In each organization, I tried to interview the person most involved in congressional lobbying. The director of each organization was sent a letter providing a brief description of my research and identifying me. For the most part, I interviewed either the director of the organization or the legislative director. In no case was I refused an interview. Some, perhaps most, of those whom I interviewed seemed to enjoy the opportunity to reflect on their work. With one exception, all the interviews lasted between sixty and ninety minutes. The one exception was an abbreviated interview of twenty minutes. All the subjects were asked if I could attribute their remarks to them. Only one person did not want to be attributed by name.

All the interviews followed a standardized format. This format was used in order to facilitate comparison and reveal generalizations in the form of political perceptions and behavior. While conducting each interview, I occasionally desired additional flexibility to probe more deeply in a particular area. It is my hope that the more uniform format will provided broader explanations, although there is some sacrifice in the depth of understanding of each individual organization. Each of the interviews was tape-recorded. Many of the subjects expressed gratitude that I was taping the interview because it would facilitate more accurate quotes. After asking their permission to tape the interview, I placed the recorder so that they could not see the revolving tape. My hope was that this placement would make the recorder less intrusive. Though it is difficult to comment on the impact of the recorder, it was my impression that each respondent virtually forgot about it. Each tape was later transcribed.

At each interview, additional data were gathered by asking for any printed information that would give more information about the organization. Some respondents volunteered information before they were asked. These data varied from group to group; they consisted of newsletters, brochures, annual reports, photocopies of press clippings and more lengthy books or booklets describing the philosophy of each organization. In addition to this rather unsystematic collection, I also asked each group to fill out a brief survey and mail it to me at their convenience. This survey solicited basic quantitative information about the organization's budget and staff. These survey data supplement the more extensive interview data.

NOTES

CHAPTER 1

1. Quoted in Richard John Neuhaus, "The Naked Public Square," in Richard McMunn, ed., *Religion in Politics* (Milwaukee: Catholic League for Religious and Civil Rights), pp. 79–80.

2. Commenting on the print media, historian and journalist Garry Wills observes that, "Editors seem to prefer inarticulacy on the subject. Major papers and networks encourage reporters to acquire expertise in the law or economics, but I have not heard of any editor asking reporters to brush up on their theology." Wills argues further that to ignore the role of religion in public life is to fail to understand the complete picture. "If we neglect the religious element in all those struggles, we cannot understand our own corporate past; we cannot even talk meaningfully to each other about things that will affect us all." Garry Wills, *Under God: Religion and Politics in America* (New York: Simon and Schuster, 1990), pp. 18 & 25.

3. Phillip E. Hammond, ed., *The Sacred in a Secular Age* (Berkeley: University of California Press, 1985), p. 1.

4. Robert N. Bellah, *Beyond Belief* (New York: Harper & Row, 1970), p. 237.

5. Kenneth D. Wald, *Religion and Politics in the United States*, 2nd ed. (Washington, DC: CQ Press, 1992), p. 14.

6. A look at social science literature reveals at least a de facto acceptance of secularization theory. Benson and Williams argue that social scientists have ignored the role of religion in public affairs for twenty years. In the political science literature between 1983 and 1987 (summer), only one article in the major journals (*American Political Science Review, Journal of Politics, American Journal of Political Science, Political Science Quarterly,* and *Western Political Quarterly*) analyzed the role of religion in a major way. Peter L. Benson and Dorothy L. Williams, *Religion on Capitol Hill* (New York: Oxford University Press, 1986), p. 5.

7. See Allen D. Hertzke, "American Religion and Politics: A Review Essay," *Western Political Quarterly* 41 (December 1988): 825–38; and James L. Guth et al., "The Politics of Religion in America: Issues for Investigation," *American Politics Quarterly* 16:118–59, for helpful reviews of recent research in the discipline of political science.

8. Martha Sawyer Allen, "Our Fight Is Righteous," *Star Tribune: Newspaper of the Twin Cities,* December 10, 1993, p. 18A.

9. Cf. John Leo, "Hillary from the Pulpit," *U.S. News and World Report,* June 7, 1993, p. 20.

10. Cf. Allen D. Hertzke, *Echoes of Discontent: Jesse Jackson, Pat Robertson, and the Resurgence of Populism* (Washington, DC: CQ Press, 1993), pp. 135–50 for a fuller discussion of the relationship between Pat Robertson's organization and the Republican party.

11. "Read and Run: A Cram Course for the Presidency," *New York Times Book Review,* June 5, 1988, p. 39. In this

quote, Molly Yard was referring to the Roman Catholic Church.

12. David S. Broder, "Church, State, and Politics," *Washington Post Weekly Edition*, January 3, 1988, p. 4.

13. James Davison Hunter, *Culture Wars: The Struggle to Define America* (New York: Basic Books, 1991); and Robert Wuthnow, *The Restructuring of American Religion: Society and Faith since World War II* (Princeton, NJ: Princeton University Press, 1988).

14. Robert Booth Fowler, *Religion and Politics in America* (Metuchen, NJ: Scarecrow Press, 1985); James L. Guth and John C. Green, eds., *The Bible and the Ballot Box: Religion and Politics in the 1988 Election* (Boulder, CO: Westview Press, 1991); Allen Hertzke, *Representing God in Washington: The Role of Religious Lobbies* (Knoxville: University of Tennessee Press, 1988); Ted G. Jelen, ed., *Religion and Political Behavior in the United States* (New York: Praeger, 1989); David C. Leege and Lyman A. Kellstedt, eds., *Rediscovering the Religious Factor in American Politics* (Armonk, NY: M. E. Sharpe, 1993); Michael Lienesch, *Redeeming America: Piety and Politics in the New Christian Right* (Chapel Hill: University of North Carolina Press, 1993); Matthew C. Moen, *The Christian Right and Congress* (Tuscaloosa: University of Alabama Press, 1989); Matthew C. Moen, *The Transformation of the Christian Right* (Tuscaloosa: University of Alabama Press, 1993); A. James Reichley, *Religion in American Public Life* (Washington, DC: Brookings Institution, 1985); Kenneth D. Wald, *Religion and Politics in the United States* (New York: St. Martin's, 1987) and *Religion and Politics in the United States*, 2nd ed. (Washington, DC: CQ Press, 1992); Clyde Wilcox, *God's Warriors: The Christian Right in Twentieth-Century America* (Baltimore: Johns Hopkins University Press, 1992). Only the Hertzke book is exclusively about religious inter-

est groups. Many of the other books include treatments of the role of religious interest groups.

15. For a discussion of the autonomy of religion in different countries including the United States, cf. Matthew C. Moen and Lowell S. Gustafson, eds., *The Religious Challenge to the State* (Philadelphia: Temple University Press, 1992).

16. Wills, *Under God*, p. 380.

17. In the United States there is a small community of believers outside of the Christian and Jewish traditions. For the most part, they are inactive in Washington politics. One exception is the American Muslim Council, which is a member of Interfaith IMPACT.

18. Max Weber, *The Sociology of Religion*, 4th ed., trans. Ephraim Fischoff (Boston: Beacon Press, 1964, originally published 1922), pp. 46–59.

19. David L. Peterson, "Ways of Thinking about Israel's Prophets," in David L. Petersen, ed., *Prophecy in Israel* (Philadelphia: Fortress Press, 1987), p. 14.

20. Sigmund Mowinckel, "Cult and Prophecy," in Petersen, *Prophecy in Israel*, pp. 74–98.

21. For a fuller discussion of the creation of an association of prophets institutionalized as fully as priests see B. D. Napier, "Prophet," in *The Interpreters' Dictionary of the Bible*, K–Q (Nashville, TN: Abingdon Press, 1962), 896–920.

22. For a fuller discussion of this issue, cf. Mark Chaves, "Intraorganizational Power and Internal Secularization in Protestant Denominations." *American Journal of Sociology* 99 (No. 1, July 1993): 1–48.

23. Cited in *Right-Wing Watch,* a publication of People for the American Way, 4, no. 1 (October 1993):1.

24. Rev. Jim Sessions, cited in *ACTION,* a pamphlet of Interfaith IMPACT, 3, no. 18 (November 10, 1993):1.

25. See James L. Guth et al., "The Politics of Religion in America: Issues for Investigation," *American Politics Quarterly* 16:376, for a discussion of the lack of research in the internal politics of religious interest groups and institutions.

26. Luke Ebersole, *Church Lobbying in the Nation's Capitol* (New York: Macmillan, 1951); Paul Blanshard, *God and Man in Washington* (Boston: Beacon Press, 1960); James Luther Adams, *The Growing Church Lobby in Washington* (Grand Rapids, MI: Eerdmans, 1970).

27. E. E. Schattschneider, *The Semisovereign People: A Realist's View of Democracy in America,* 2nd ed. (Hinsdale, IL: Dryden Press, 1975, originally published in 1962).

28. Grant McConnell, *Private Power and American Democracy* (New York: Norton, 1966).

29. Theodore Lowi, *The End of Liberalism,* 2nd ed. (New York: Norton, 1979).

30. Theodore J. Lowi, "New Dimensions in Policy and Politics," in Raymond Tatalovich and Byron W. Daynes, eds., *Social Regulatory Policy: Moral Controversies in American Politics* (Boulder, CO: Westview Press, 1988), p. xx.

31. Virginia Sapiro, "Research Frontier Essay: When Are Interests Interesting? The Problem of Political Representation of Women," *American Political Science Review* 75, no. 3 (September 1981): 701–16.

32. Wald, *Religion and Politics in the United States,* 2nd ed., p. 26.

33. Allen Hertzke has also worked to define the religious interest. In his study, he asked religious lobbyists the question "Whom or what do you represent?" From the responses, Hertzke divided the representational roles of religion into four categories: institutional concerns, domestic constituencies, theological traditions, and international constituencies. Hertzke, *Representing God in Washington,* pp. 94–116.

34. George Gallup, Jr., and Jim Castelli, *The People's Religion* (New York: Macmillan, 1989), p. 16.

35. Peter Steinfels, "New Law Protects Religious Practices," *New York Times,* November 17, 1993, p. A18.

36. Cf. Jeffrey M. Berry, *Lobbying for the People: The Political Behavior of Public Interest Groups* (Princeton, NJ: Princeton University Press, 1977), pp. 298–300. Berry places religious groups in his sample of public interest groups. More general studies of interest groups, such as Kay Lehman Schlozman and John Tierney, *Organized Interests and American Democracy* (New York: Harper & Row, 1986), place religious interest groups in other categories with other public interest organizations.

37. Isaiah 2:4.

38. Amos 5:24.

39. Luke 4:18.

40. Robert Wuthnow, *The Restructuring of American Religion* (Princeton, NJ: Princeton University Press, 1988), pp. 317–18.

41. Ibid., p. 318.

42. See Robert S. Bachelder, "Blinded by Metaphor: Churches and Welfare Reform," *Christian Century* 105 (December 14, 1988): 1147–49; and Patrick Conover, "Welfare and Workfare: A Dispute," *Christian Century* 106 (April 19, 1989): 419–21.

43. Hertzke, *Echoes of Discontent*, p. 208. Hertzke uses data from the 1988 American National Election Study, Survey Research Center-Center for Political Studies, University of Michigan, Ann Arbor, 1988.

44. The vagueness of the concept "religious interest" is analogous to the imprecision of the concept "public interest." While politicians do not agree on the definition of the public interest, scholars have developed operational definitions of public interest groups. These operational definitions serve to delineate the scope of the study of public interest groups. The most common definition is any group seeking benefits or a collective good that will not selectively benefit the membership or the activists of the organization. Berry, *Lobbying for the People*, p. 7; Schlozman and Tierney, *Organized Interests and American Democracy*, p. 29. Cf. Frank J. Sorauf, "The Public Interest Reconsidered," *Journal of Politics* 19 (1957): 616–39, for a discussion of the use of the concept "public interest" in political analysis.

45. See Appendix for a fuller discussion of my methodology and sample.

46. Schlozman and Tierney, *Organized Interests and American Democracy*, p. 10.

47. Paul J. Weber and T. L. Stanley, "The Power and Performance of Religious Interest Groups," *Quarterly Review* 4 (1984): 28.

48. Paul J. Weber and W. Landis Jones, *U.S. Religious Interest Groups: Institutional Profiles* (Westport, CT: Greenwood Press, 1994).

49. Although they do not state a clear definition, this seems to be the approach of Allen Hertzke and Robert Zwier in two recent studies of religious interest groups: Hertzke, *Representing God in Washington;* and Robert Zwier, "The World and Worldview of Religious Lobbyists," paper presented at the 1988 meeting of the Midwest Political Science Association, Chicago, April 4–6.

CHAPTER 2

1. Wolfgang Schluchter, "The Future of Religion," in *Culture and Society: Contemporary Debates*, ed. Jeffrey C. Alexander and Steven Seidman (New York: Cambridge University Press, 1990) p. 256.

2. Quoted in Schluchter, "The Future of Religion," p. 255. See also Peter Iver Kaufman, *Redeeming Politics* (Princeton, NJ: Princeton University Press, 1990), ch. 5, for a more nuanced discussion of the role of the papacy in medieval politics. The title of the chapter is "The Imperial Papacy."

3. See Kaufman, *Redeeming Politics*, ch. 6, for a more complete discussion of John Calvin's Geneva.

4. Quoted in Sydney Mead, *The Old Religion in the Brave New World: Reflections on the Relationship Between Christendom and the Republic* (Berkeley: University of California Press, 1977), pp. 49–50.

5. Perry Miller, ed., *The American Puritans* (New York: Anchor Books, 1956), p. 83.

6. Cushing Strout, *The New Heavens and New Earth: Political Religion in America* (New York: Harper & Row, 1974), p. 14.

7. Theda Skocpol, "Bringing the State Back In: Strategies of Analysis in Current Research," in *Bringing the State Back In,* ed. Peter B. Evans, Dietrich Rueschemeyer, and Theda Skocpol (New York: Cambridge University Press, 1985), p. 28.

8. Sydney Ahlstrom, "The Puritan Ethic and the Spirit of American Democracy," in *Calvinism and the Political Order,* ed. George L. Hunt (Philadelphia: Westminster Press, 1965), p. 95.

9. The following discussion of the Quaker movement in Pennsylvania relies heavily on A. James Reichley, *Religion in American Public Life* (Washington, DC: Brookings Institution, 1985).

10. Quoted in Strout, *The New Heavens and New Earth,* p. 23.

11. Albert C. Applegarth, *Quakers in Pennsylvania* (Johns Hopkins, 1892), p. 34, quoted in Reichley, *Religion in American Public Life,* p. 80.

12. Cf. Jean R. Soderlund, ed., *William Penn and the Founding of Pennsylvania: 1680–1684, A Documentary History* (Philadelphia: University of Pennsylvania Press, 1983), pp. 74, 84, 307–345.

13. Martin E. Marty, *Pilgrims in Their Own Land: 500 Years of Religion in America* (Boston: Little, Brown, 1984), p. 88.

14. To be sure, the Quakers were not absolute. "They grew adept at the politics of shuffle and evasion, but in the end they usually found ways to meet the military demands. The

usual formula was to grant money 'for the Queen's use.' No
one was deceived as to the use the Queen would make of
the money. But, as one of the leading Quaker politicians put
it, 'We did not see it to be inconsistent with our principles
to give the Queen money notwithstanding any use she
might put it to that being not our part but hers.'" Frederick
B. Tolles, *Quakerism and the Atlantic Culture* (New York:
Macmillan, 1947), p. 50.

15. Strout, *The New Heavens and New Earth*, p. 20.

16. Quoted in Martin E. Marty, *Anticipating Pluralism: The
Founders' Vision* (Providence, RI: Associates of the John Carter Brown Library, 1986), p. 1.

17. Cf. Sydney E. Ahlstrom, *A Religious History of the American People* (New Haven, CT: Yale University Press, 1972), p.
182.

18. Cf. Marty, *Anticipating Pluralism*.

19. Interestingly, the disestablishment of churches in America seems to have contributed to the vitality of organized
religion. In contrast to Europe, where governments continue to support state churches, religion in the United States
has remained much more active. Poll data show the increased importance of religion in the United States. The
Gallup organization collected data in the United States and
the major European countries on six questions concerning
religion: weekly church attendance, belief in a personal
God, importance of God in daily life, belief in life after
death, obtaining comfort from religion, and whether the
church in each country answers people's spiritual needs. A
combined index of these six questions showed that only in
the Republic of Ireland was religion more important than

the United States. George Gallup, Jr., and Jim Castelli, *The People's Religion* (New York: Macmillan, 1989), p. 47.

20. In Reichley, *Religion in American Public Life*, pp. 101–4.

21. Ibid., pp. 111–12.

22. Ibid., p. 107.

23. James Madison, Alexander Hamilton, and John Jay, *The Federalist Papers* (New York: Penguin Books, 1987), p. 128.

24. Cf. Garry Wills, *Under God: Religion and Politics in America* (New York: Simon and Schuster, 1990).

25. Cf. George Forell, *Faith Active in Love* (Minneapolis: Augsburg, 1964), for a fuller discussion of Lutheran theology.

26. Sydney Ahlstrom, *A Religious History of the American People* (New Haven, CT, and London: Yale University Press, 1972), p. 667.

27. Cf. Robert Booth Fowler, *Religion and Politics in America* (Metuchen, NJ: Scarecrow Press, 1985), pp. 94–96, for a fuller discussion.

28. George M. Marsden, *Fundamentalism and American Culture: The Shaping of Twentieth Century Evangelism, 1870–1925* (New York: Oxford University Press, 1980), pp. 36–37.

29. Frances Fitzgerald, "A Disciplined, Charging Army," *New Yorker*, May 18, 1981, p. 63.

30. Matthew C. Moen, "The Christian Right in the United States," in Matthew C. Moen and Lowell S. Gustafson, eds.,

The Religious Challenge to the State (Philadelphia: Temple University Press, 1992), pp. 76–82.

31. Romans 13:1, See also 1 Peter 2:10 and Titus 3:1.

32. Martin Luther, "Secular Authority—To What Extent Should It Be Obeyed," in J. M. Porter, ed., *Luther: Selected Political Writings* (Philadelphia: Fortress Press, 1974).

33. Richard John Neuhaus, *The Naked Public Square: Religion and Democracy in America* (New York: Harper & Row, 1984), p. 116.

34. Institute for Religion and Democracy, pamphlet.

35. H. Richard Niebuhr, *Christ and Culture* (New York: Harper and Brothers, 1951).

36. The classic formulation of civil religion is Robert N. Bellah, "Civil Religion in America," *Daedalus* 96 (Winter 1967): 1–21.

37. Kenneth D. Wald, *Religion and Politics in the United States* (New York: St. Martin's, 1987), p. 51.

38. Cf. Sidney E. Mead, "The Post-Protestant Concept and America's Two Religions," in Martin E. Marty, ed., *Civil Religion Church and State* (New York: K. G. Saur, 1992), p. 103.

39. Cf. Bellah et al., *Habits of the Heart*, pp. 28–29.

40. Cf. Cynthia Toolin, "American Civil Religion from 1979–1981: A Content Analysis of Presidential Inaugural Addresses," *Review of Religious Research* 25:39–48, for a discussion of the religious language of presidential inaugural addresses.

41. Cited in David Howard-Pitney, *The Afro-American Jeremiad: Appeals for Justice in America* (Philadelphia: Temple University Press, 1992), p. 6.

42. Fred Barnes, "The New Covenant: Clinton's Religious Strategy," *The New Republic* 207 (No. 9, 1992, n20): 32–34.

43. Cf. Robert Wood Lynn, "Civil Catechetics in Mid-Victorian America: Some Notes about American Civil Religion, Past and Present," *Religious Education* 68(1973): 5–27.

44. Another example of this support is found in Robert Wuthnow's book *The Restructuring of American Religion* (Princeton, NJ: Princeton University Press, 1988), p. 3. Wuthnow recounts the story of a Sunday school parade on June 6, 1946, in Brooklyn. The purpose of the event was to commemorate the second anniversary of the Normandy invasion and to give thanks and reflect on the heritage of America. Ninety thousand students attended. The mayor of Brooklyn and governor of New York were in the reviewing stand.

45. Ibid., p. 244.

46. Howard-Pitney, *The Afro-American Jeremiad*, p. 20.

47. Quoted in James Luther Adams, *The Growing Church Lobby in Washington* (Grand Rapids, MI: Eerdmans, 1970), p. 10.

48. Robert N. Bellah and Phillip E. Hammond, *Varieties of Civil Religion* (San Francisco: Harper & Row, 1980), p. 20.

49. Matthew C. Moen, *The Christian Right and Congress* (Tuscaloosa: University of Alabama Press, 1989).

50. Steve Bruce, *The Rise and Fall of the New Christian Right: Conservative and Protestant Politics in America, 1978–1988* (New York: Oxford University Press, 1988).

51. Much of the following discussion draws from Wuthnow, *The Restructuring of American Religion*, pp. 244–57.

52. Jerry Falwell, *Fundamentalist Phenomenon: The Resurgence of Conservative Christianity* (Garden City, NY: Doubleday, 1981), quoted in Wuthnow, *The Restructuring of American Religion*, p. 247.

53. Wuthnow, *The Restructuring of American Religion*, p. 250.

54. Donald E. Miller, "The Future of Liberal Christianity," *Christian Century* 10 (March 1982): 266.

55. National Conference of Catholic Bishops, *Economic Justice for All: Pastoral Letter on Catholic Social Teaching and the U.S. Economy* (Washington, D.C.: 1986), paragraph 34.

56. For a more complete analysis of the bishops' letter on the economy, see Daniel J.B. Hofrenning, "The General Welfare and Public Policy: An Analysis of the Debate among American Catholics," unpublished manuscript, 1991.

57. Mark 8:34–35.

58. Luke 4:18, 6:24, 12:13–21, 16:19–31.

59. Proverbs 28:11; Amos 5:4–13; Isaiah 2:6–8.

60. Revelation 21:1–4; Isaiah 11:6, 25:1–8.

61. George A. Chauncey, "Faith and Politics: The Differences," in *Reformed Faith and Politics*, ed. Ronald Stone

(Washington, DC: University Press of America, 1983), pp. 28–29.

62. See Robert Bellah, *The Broken Covenant: American Civil Religion in a Time of Trial* (New York: Seabury Press, 1975).

CHAPTER 3

1. Arthur F. Bentley, *The Process of Government* (Chicago: University of Chicago Press, 1908).

2. David B. Truman, *The Governmental Process* (New York: Knopf, 1951).

3. Ibid., p. 104.

4. Ibid., pp. 28ff. See also Daniel J.B. Hofrenning, "Into the Public Square: The Origins of Religious Interest Groups," *Social Science Journal* 32 (1995): 35–48.

5. As noted in Chapter 1, many critics of pluralism contend that analysis should focus not on active groups but on those that have not yet organized. From this perspective, the most important dimension of the policy process is not the bargaining and compromising of organized interests; instead, it is the suppression of potential interests by the ruling elite. Because many interests are not represented at the bargaining table where public policy is produced, the pluralist view of public policy is viewed as illegitimate. To counter elite domination, these theorists move beyond the pluralist focus on interest groups and propose political parties, a strong president, and social movements as antidotes to elite domination. Few political scientists have focused on interest groups as a source of antielitist pressure.

6. To be sure, religious lobbyists are not the only organizations seeking fundamental change. Feminist, environ-

mental, labor, and other more ideological organizations also seek far-reaching changes. Thus we should expect them to behave in ways similar to religious lobbyists. The data in Chapter 5 provide a limited comparison of religious organizations, labor unions, and public interest groups; however, the primary comparison in this project is between religious and nonreligious lobbyists. Hopefully, future scholars can build upon my work and develop a more nuanced disaggregation of the data.

7. Theodore J. Lowi, "American Business, Public Policy, Case-Studies, and Political Theory," *World Politics* 16 (1964): 677–715.

8. Ibid., p. 680.

9. Earl Latham, "The Group Basis of Politics," in Heinz Eulau, Samuel J. Eldersveld, and Morris Janowitz, eds., *Political Behavior* (New York: Free Press, 1956), p. 239.

10. Charles Lindblom, "The Science of 'Muddling Through,'" *Public Administration Review* 19 (1959): 83–88.

11. See *ibid.* 79–88, and "Still Muddling, Not Yet Through," *Public Administration Review* 39 (1979): 517–26, for a fuller description of Lindblom's notion of incremental change.

12. Cf. Kay Lehman Schlozman and John Tierney, *Organized Interests and American Democracy* (New York: Harper & Row, 1986), and Ronald J. Hrebenar and Ruth K. Scott, *Interest Group Politics in America*, 2nd ed., (Englewood Cliffs, NJ: Prentice Hall, 1990).

13. Schlozman and Tierney make a similar distinction using different terms. Indirect tactics are covered in a chapter entitled "Reaching Out to the Public." Direct tactics are cov-

ered in a chapter entitled "Approaching Government Directly." See *Organized Interests and American Democracy*, chs. 8 and 11. In yet another way, Ornstein and Elder use the terms "insider" and "outsider lobbying." See Norman J. Ornstein and Shirley Elder, *Interest Groups, Lobbying and Public Policy* (Washington, DC: Congressional Quarterly, 1978).

14. Ibid., pp. 89ff.

15. Ibid., pp. 69ff.

16. See W. Phillips Shively, *Power and Choice: An Introduction to Political Science*, 3rd ed. (New York: Random House, 1993), pp. 97–98, for a discussion of the distinction between incremental and radical politics.

17. Theodore J. Lowi, "Foreword: New Dimensions in Policy and Politics," in Raymond Tatalovich and Byron W. Daynes, eds., *Social Regulatory Policy: Moral Controversies in American Politics* (Boulder, CO: Westview Press, 1988), pp. xii–xiv.

18. Ibid., p. xii.

19. Ibid., p. xx.

20. See Herbert McCloskey, Paul Hoffman, and Rosemary O'Hara, "Issue Conflict and Consensus among Party Leaders and Followers," *American Political Science Review* 54 (1960): 406–27; John Jackson, B. Brown, and D. Bositis, "Herbert McCloskey and Friends Revisited," *American Politics Quarterly* 10 (1982): 158–80; and Warren Miller and M. Kent Jennings, *Parties in Transition: A Longitudinal Study of Party Elites and Party Supporters* (New York: Russell Sage, 1987), for additional work in this theme.

21. Aaron Wildavsky, "The Goldwater Phenomenon: Purists, Politicians, and the Two-Party System," *Review of Politics* 27 (1965): 395.

22. Jeane Kirkpatrick, *The New Presidential Elite* (New York: Russell Sage, 1976).

23. Wildavsky, "The Goldwater Phenomenon," p. 396.

24. Ibid., p. 397.

25. See James L. Guth and John C. Green, "The Moralizing Minority: Christian Right Support among Political Contributors," in Ted G. Jelen, ed., *Religion and Political Behavior in the United States* (New York: Praeger, 1989), pp. 223–41.

26. Robert Michels, *Political Parties* (New York: Collier Books, 1962, published originally in 1915).

27. Cf. Lewis A. Coser, "Introduction" in Lewis A. Coser, ed., *George Simmel* (Englewood Cliffs, NJ: Prentice Hall, 1965).

28. Mancur Olson, *The Logic of Collective Action* (Cambridge, MA: Harvard University Press, 1965).

29. See Larry Rothenberg, "Choosing among Public Interest Groups: Membership, Activism and Retention in Political Organizations," *American Political Science Review* 82 (1988): 1129–52, for a more complete explanation of the decision by members to retain their membership.

30. See James Guth et al., *The Politics of Religion in America*, pp. 374–75, for a discussion of "by-product" lobbying among religious lobbyists.

31. Aaron Wildavsky, *The Nursing Father: Moses as a Political Leader* (Tuscaloosa: University of Alabama Press, 1984).

32. James Wood, *Leadership in Voluntary Associations* (New Brunswick, NJ: Rutgers University Press, 1984).

33. J. Elliott Corbett, "Should the Church Lobby?" *Engage,* October 15, 1970, pp. 6, 8.

34. See Sydney Ahlstrom, *A Religious History of the American People* (New Haven, CT: Yale University Press, 1972), pp. 382–383, for a discussion of the voluntaristic character of American churches in colonial America.

35. See Seymour Martin Lipset, Martin Trow, and James Coleman, *Union Democracy: The Inside Politics of the International Typographical Union* (New York: Free Press, 1956), cited in Schlozman and Tierney, *Organized Interests and American Democracy,* p. 138.

36. See Schlozman and Tierney, *Organized Interests and American Democracy,* pp. 133ff., and Maurice Duverger, *Political Parties* (New York: Wiley, 1963), p. 135.

37. Olson, *The Logic of Collective Action,* p. 160.

38. Robert S. Salisbury, "An Exchange Theory of Interest Groups," *Midwest Journal of Political Science* 13 (February 1969): 1–32. See also Peter B. Clark and James Q. Wilson, "Incentive Systems: A Theory of Organizations," *Administrative Science Quarterly* 6 (September 1961): 129–66; and James Q. Wilson, *Political Organizations* (New York: Basic Books, 1973).

39. Albert Hirschman, *Exit, Voice, and Loyalty* (Cambridge, MA: Harvard University Press, 1970).

40. Paul A. Sabatier and Susan M. McGlaughlin, "Belief Congruence between Interest-Group Leaders and Mem-

bers," *Journal of Politics* 52 (August 1990): 916; Terry M. Moe, "Toward a Broader Theory of Interest Groups, *Journal of Politics* 43 (1981): 543.

41. John Mark Hansen, "The Political Economy of Group Membership," *American Political Science Review* 79 (1985): 80.

42. Richard F. Fenno, Jr., *Congressmen in Committees* (Boston: Scott, Foresman, 1973).

43. David E. Price, "Policymaking in Congressional Committees: The Impact of 'Environmental Factors,'" *American Political Science Review* 71 (March 1977): 548.

44. George Gallup, Jr., and Jim Castelli, *The People's Religion* (New York: Macmillan, 1989), p. 233.

45. Ibid., p. 139.

46. For a parallel argument concerning the political behavior of legislators see R. Kent Weaver, "The Politics of Blame Avoidance," *Journal of Public Policy* 6 (1986): 371–98.

CHAPTER 4

1. See George Gallup, Jr., and Jim Castelli, *The People's Religion* (New York: Macmillan, 1989), p. 16.

2. See Robert Salisbury, "Overlapping Memberships, Organizational Interactions and Interest Group Theory," paper presented at the 1976 meeting of the American Political Science Association, cited in Ronald J. Hrebenar and Ruth K. Scott, *Interest Group Politics in America* (Englewood Cliffs, NJ: Prentice Hall, 1982), p. 30. Salisbury notes that the next most frequently joined groups are sports groups and school

service groups such as the PTA; 17.5 percent of the population belong to such groups.

3. Sixteen percent work in professional/technical and managerial/administrative positions. Kay Lehman Schlozman and John Tierney, *Organized Interests and American Democracy* (New York: Harper & Row, 1986), p. 70.

4. James Q. Wilson, *Political Organizations* (New York: Basic Books, 1973), p. 60.

5. See Sidney Verba and Norman H. Nie, *Participation in America* (New York: Harper & Row, 1972), chapter 8, and Allen Hertzke, *Representing God in Washington: The Role of Religious Lobbies* (Knoxville: University of Tennessee Press, 1988), p. 14.

6. Quoted in Hertzke, *Representing God in Washington*, p. 12.

7. Stephen Engelberg with Martin Tolchin, "Foreigners Find New Ally Is U.S. Industry," *New York Times*, November 2, 1993, p. A1.

8. Cf. Schlozman and Tierney, *Organized Interests and American Democracy*, p. 93.

9. Luke 1:51–53.

10. Will Herberg, *Protestant-Catholic-Jew* (New York: Doubleday, 1955).

11. Kenneth D. Wald, "Assessing the Religious Factor in Electoral Behavior," in *Religion in American Politics*, ed. Charles W. Dunn (Washington, DC: CQ Press, 1989), p. 108.

12. Gallup and Castelli, *The People's Religion*, pp. 27–28; and Robert Wuthnow, *The Restructuring of American Religion: So-*

ciety and Faith since World War II (Princeton, NJ: Princeton University Press, 1988), chs. 5, 8.

13. Wald, "Assessing the Religious Factor in Electoral Behavior."

14. Allen Hertzke, *Representing God in Washington*, pp. 213–16.

15. A. James Reichley, *Religion in American Public Life* (Washington, DC: Brookings Institution, 1985), p. 312.

16. Kenneth D. Wald, *Religion and Politics in the United States* (New York: St. Martin's, 1987), p. 200.

17. Cf. Paul J. Achtemeier, ed., *Harper's Bible Dictionary* (San Francisco: Harper & Row, 1985), p. 286.

18. Cf. Stephen L. Carter, *The Culture of Disbelief: How American Law and Politics Trivialize Religious Devotion* (New York: Basic Books, 1993), for a fuller discussion of this topic.

19. Cf. Matthew C. Moen, *The Christian Right and Congress* (Tuscaloosa: University of Alabama Press, 1989).

20. Cf. Sidney Blumenthal, "Christian Soldiers," *The New Yorker* 70 (July 18, 1994): 31 and Robert Sullivan, "An Army of the Faithful," *New York Times Mgazine* (April 25, 1993): 32.

21. Pat Robertson, "Dear Christian Friend" letter written to members of Christian Coalition.

22. "Christian Coalition Congressional Scorecard," Christian Coalition, Chesapeake Bay, VA, 1993.

23. Robert H. Salisbury, "Interest Representation: The Dominance of Institutions," *American Political Science Review* 78 (1984): 75.

24. Ibid., p. 67.

25. Ibid.

26. Ibid., p. 68.

27. The bylaws of most Protestant conventions call for a convention makeup of 50 percent clergy and 50 percent lay delegates. Since lay members vastly outnumber the clergy, it is clear that the process is not a pure democracy.

CHAPTER 5

1. Abraham J. Heschel, *The Prophets,* vol. 1 (New York: Harper & Row, 1962), p. 5.

2. Walter Brueggemann, *The Prophetic Imagination* (Philadelphia: Fortress Press, 1978), p. 13.

3. Ibid., p. 16.

4. Ibid., p. 13.

5. Allen Hertzke, *Representing God in Washington: The Role of Religious Lobbies in the American Polity,* p. 203.

6. Heschel, *The Prophets,* vol. 1, p. 9.

7. See Steve Bruce, *The Rise and Fall of the New Christian Right: Conservative and Protestant Politics in America, 1978–1988* (New York: Oxford University Press, 1988), for a description of the factors that caused the mobilization of conservative Christians.

8. Kim A. Lawton, "The Family Man," *Christianity Today* 36, no. 13 (November 9, 1992): 26.

9. Interview with Peter Waldron, consultant, Moral Majority, June 1989.

10. Jerry Falwell, *Listen America* (Garden City, NY: Doubleday, 1980).

11. "Moral Majority Won't Return, but Falwell Stays in Politics," *Church and State* 46, no. 9 (October 1993): 15–16.

12. Christian Voice, "Preserving a Free Society," pamphlet.

13. Interview with John Carr, secretary of social development and world peace, U.S. Catholic Conference, November 1988.

14. Interview with Gretchen Eick, director, IMPACT, November 1988.

15. Interview with Patrick Conovor, policy advocate, United Church of Christ, November 1988.

16. Interview with Bob Tiller, director, Office of Governmental Relations, American Baptist Churches USA, November 1988.

17. Nancy Sylvester, NETWORK national coordinator, membership letter.

18. Interview with Sally Timmel, coordinator, Church Women United, June 1988.

19. Interview with Ed Snyder, executive secretary, Friends Committee for National Legislation, November 1988.

20. Interview with Glen Stein, associate director, Union of American Hebrew Congregations, November 1988.

21. Richard A. Viguerie, *The New Right: We're Ready to Lead* (Falls Church, VA: The Viguerie Company, 1981), p. 107.

22. Interview with Matthew Davis Smyth, legislative director, Christian Voice, June 1989.

23. Interview with Peter Waldron, consultant, Moral Majority, June 1989.

24. Moral Majority brochure, 1983, cited in Bruce, *The Rise and Fall of the New Christian Right*, p. 81.

25. Interview with Gary Bauer, president of the Family Research Council, in "Focus on the Family: A Vigorous Voice in Washington," *Citizen* 3 (January 1989): 14–15. (Focus on the Family is the name of the organization that published *Citizen*.)

26. Interview with Matthew Davis Smyth, legislative director, Christian Voice, June 1989.

27. For a vivid sense of the Christian conservatives' disillusionment with the Reagan administration, see Peter E. Waldron, *Rebuilding the Walls: A Biblical Strategy for Restoring America's Greatness* (Brentwood, TN: Wogemuth & Hyatt, 1987), ch. 2. The chapter is titled "The Conservative Betrayal."

28. See Matthew C. Moen, *The Christian Right and Congress* (Tuscaloosa: University of Alabama Press, 1989), pp. 168–69.

29. Bruce, *The Rise and Fall of the New Christian Right*.

30. Ibid., p. 182.

31. Quoted in Erin Saberi, "From Moral Majority to Organized Minority: Tactics of the Religious Right," *Christian Century,* 110 (August 11–18, 1993): 781.

32. "Building a Christian G.O.P.," *Harper's Magazine* 286, no. 1712 (January 1993): 26. See also Saberi, "From Moral Majority to Organized Minority," p. 781.

33. Interview with Robert Tiller, director, American Baptist Churches USA, November 1988.

34. See Ronald J. Hrebenar and Ruth K. Scott, *Interest Group Politics in America,* 2nd ed. (Englewood Cliffs, NJ: Prentice Hall, 1990), pp. 89–93, for a more complete discussion of lobbyists' use of informal contacts.

35. Interview with John Carr, secretary of social development and world peace, U.S. Catholic Conference, November 1988.

36. Not for attribution.

37. M. Anthony Carr and Andrew Wall, "Does America Need a New Congress," *Liberty Report,* July 1988, pp. 6–9.

38. Skipp Porteous, "Christian Coalition Update," *Free Inquiry* 12, no. 2 (Spring 1992): 16.

39. Interestingly, the recent surge in resentment against Washington does not seem to have contributed to large membership increases; liberal groups seem particularly stagnant. Although conservative groups like the Christian Coalition are growing, most (not all) liberal groups seem unable to capitalize on citizen frustration with Washington politics. Their size has remained relatively stable.

40. Stephen L. Carter, *The Culture of Disbelief: How American Law and Politics Trivialize Religious Devotion* (New York: Basic Books, 1993), p. 35.

41. Cited in ibid., p. 35.

42. Although comprehensive data are not available, this view seems to be a minority perspective among secular lobbyists. As a limited comparison, William Browne's research does show a subset of agrarian protest groups who "desire sweeping reform in either food production or farm programs." But protest groups are only a small part of the larger universe of contemporary agricultural groups. In a universe of 129 organizations in Browne's study, only ten were identified as protest organizations, and some of those organizations did not focus much energy on national politics. William P. Browne, *Private Interests, Public Policy, and American Agriculture* (Lawrence: University Press of Kansas, 1988), pp. 58, 253–56. See ch. 4 for a fuller description of agrarian protest groups.

43. Interview with Arthur Keys, executive director, Interfaith Action for Economic Justice, November 1988.

44. Church Women United, "Piecing Together," pamphlet.

45. Presbyterian Church (U.S.A.), Washington Office, pamphlet, May 1988.

46. Interview with Nancy Sylvester, national coordinator, NETWORK, November 1988.

47. 1971 Synod, *Justice in the World,* quoted in Catholic Charities U.S.A., "Legislative Program for the 100th Congress," booklet.

48. United States Catholic Conference, *Political Responsibility: Choices for the Future,* booklet, September 1987.

49. Concerned Women for America, "Come Help Save America," pamphlet.

50. Interview with Sally White, legislative director, Concerned Women for America, June 1989.

51. Gary Bauer, president, Family Research Council, mimeographed letter (no date).

52. Nancy Sylvester, NETWORK national coordinator, membership letter.

53. "Religious Task Force on Central America," pamphlet.

54. Interview with Gretchen Eick, director, IMPACT, November 1988.

55. See H. Richard Niebuhr, *The Kingdom of God in America* (Chicago: Willet & Clark, 1937; reprinted, New York: Harper & Row Torchbooks, 1959), for a fuller discussion of the concept in its American context.

56. Interview with James Matlack, Executive Director, American Friends Service Committee, November 1988.

57. Mennonite Central Committee, "Washington Memo," November–December, 1987.

58. Robert L. Nelson, John P. Heinz, Edward O. Laumann, and Robert H. Salisbury, "Private Representation in Washington: Surveying the Structure of Influence," *American Bar Foundation Research Journal* 177 (1987): 141–200.

59. Hugh Heclo, "Issue Networks and the Executive Establishment," in Anthony King, ed., *The New American Political System* (Washington, DC: American Enterprise Institute, 1978).

60. NETWORK, pamphlet.

61. Interfaith Action for Economic Justice, 1987 annual report, p. 3.

62. See Robert Zwier, "Coalition Strategies of Religious Interest Groups," in Ted G. Jelen, ed., *Religion and Political Behavior in the United States* (New York: Praeger, 1989), pp. 171–86.

63. *Bread for the World Newsletter* 2 (March 21, 1990): 1.

64. Interview with Stan Hasty, associate director, Baptist Joint Committee for Public Affairs, November 1988.

65. Mennonite Central Committee, "Washington Memo," November–December 1987.

66. "Religious Freedom Bill OK'd," *Christian Century* 110, no. 32 (November 10, 1993): 1116.

67. William P. Browne, "Issue Niches and the Limits of Interest Group Influence," in Allan J. Cigler and Burdett A. Loomis, eds., *Interest Group Politics*, 3rd ed. (Washington, DC: CQ Press, 1991), p. 351.

68. Cf. James Q. Wilson, *The Amateur Democrat* (Chicago: University of Chicago Press, 1962).

69. Ibid., p. 3.

70. Kay Lehman Schlozman and John T. Tierney, *Organized Interests and American Democracy* (New York: Harper & Row, 1986), p. 268.

71. Interview with Peter Waldron, consultant and lobbyist, Moral Majority, June 1989.

72. Allen Hertzke, *Representing God in Washington: The Role of Religious Lobbies* (Knoxville: University of Tennessee Press, 1988), pp. 73, 75.

73. Robert Zwier, "The World and Worldview of Religious Lobbyists," paper presented at the 1988 convention of the Midwest Political Science Association, Chicago, p. 10.

74. IMPACT, "What Does the Lord Require of You," pamphlet.

75. Not for attribution.

76. Interview with John Carr, secretary of social development and world peace, U.S. Catholic Conference, November 1988.

77. Interview with Mary Jane Patterson, director, Washington Office of the Presbyterian Church, November 1988.

78. Edgar R. Trexler, "Taking the Church's Advice," *The Lutheran* 2 (January 25, 1989): 50.

79. Gretchen Eick, "Shaping a Faithful and Effective Advocacy Ministry," in *The Evangelical Lutheran Church in America and Public Policy Advocacy: Papers from a Consultation*, ed. Roy J. Enquist (Chicago: Evangelical Lutheran Church in America, 1990), pp. 46, 48 (46–49).

80. Interview with John Lillie, acting director, Washington Office of the Evangelical Lutheran Church of America, November 1988.

81. Interview with Richard Cizik, issue analyst, National Association of Evangelicals, November 1988.

82. Interview with David Harris, Washington representative, American Jewish Congress, November 1988.

83. Interview with Glen Stein, associate director, Union of American Hebrew Congregations, November 1988.

84. Interview with Mark Pelavin, associate Washington representative, American Jewish Congress, November 1988.

CHAPTER 6

1. Hedrick Smith, *The Power Game: How Washington Works* (New York: Random House, 1988), pp. 230–31.

2. Cf. John P. Heinz et al. *The Hollow Core: Private Interests in National Policy Making* (Cambridge, MA: Harvard University Press, 1993), p. 269, for a ranking by a random sample of lobbyists of the most widely known lobbyists.

3. Cf. Allen Hertzke, *Representing God in Washington: The Role of Religious Lobbies* (Knoxville: University of Tennessee Press, 1988), p. 48.

4. Interview with Ed Snyder, Friends Committee on National Legislation, November 1988.

5. For an outstanding study of how lobbyists can shape legislators interpretations of legislation, see Richard A. Smith, "Advocacy, Interpretation, and Influence in the U.S. Congress," *American Political Science Review* 78 (1984): 44–63.

6. Joel Brinkley, "Cultivating the Grass Roots to Reap Legislative Benefits," *New York Times*, November 1, 1993, p. A1.

7. See ibid., for a fuller discussion of what he calls "new-breed lobbying."

8. See Cobb and Elder, *Participation in American Politics: The Dynamics of Agenda Building*, 2nd ed. (Baltimore, MD:

Johns Hopkins University Press, 1983) chs. 1 and 7, for a more detailed description of the politics of issue expansion.

9. E. E. Schattschneider, *The Semi-Sovereign People: A Realist's View of Democracy in America*, 2nd ed. (Hinsdale, IL: Dryden Press, 1975, originally published in 1962), ch. 2.

10. In order to provide a more specific test, I replicated the questions from Schlozman's and Tierney's survey of the broader universe of interest groups. Kay Lehman Schlozman and John T. Tierney, *Organized Interests and American Democracy* (New York: Harper & Row, 1986).

11. Some studies have indicated that the impact of organized interests serving on advisory committees is much more than consultative. For example, the Health Insurance Benefits Advisory Council, which advises the Medicare program, included representatives of beneficiaries, health care institutions, insurance professionals, public health officials, and taxpayers. Judith Feder concluded that this group greatly influenced the implementation of the Medicare program. Officials from the Social Security Administration "adapted their policies to reflect the council's consensus." The path of influence is not always clear; however, service on advisory boards clearly gives one a special inside access denied to those not serving on such boards. Judith Feder, "Medicare Implementation and the Policy Process," *Journal of Health Politics, Policy and Law* 2 (1977): 175; cited in Schlozman and Tierney, *Organized Interests and American Democracy*, p. 335.

12. Schlozman and Tierney make this point in their study. Ibid., p. 149.

13. Ralph Nader, *Unsafe at Any Speed: The Designed-In Dangers of the American Automobile* (New York: Grossman, 1965).

14. Murray Edelman is the pioneer in deciphering political symbols. All subsequent work is indebted to him. Cf. Murray Edelman, *The Symbolic Uses of Politics* (Urbana: University of Illinois Press, 1985).

15. Pamela Johnston Conover and Virginia Gray, *Feminism and the New Right: Conflict over the American Family* (New York: Praeger, 1983), p. 37.

16. Ibid., p. 37.

17. Cobb and Elder, *Participation in American Politics*, p. 116.

18. Allen Hertzke notes that the Moral Majority made an intentional switch in their definition of school prayer. "We pushed school prayer three years in a row, but we framed the issue in terms of how prayer in schools is good. But some people feel that prayer in school is bad. So we learned to frame the issue in terms of 'students' rights,' so it became a constitutional issue." Hertzke, *Representing God in Washington*, p. 195.

19. Matthew C. Moen, *The Christian Right and Congress* (Tuscaloosa: University of Alabama Press, 1992), p. 130.

20. See ibid., for a more complete discussion of the symbolic strategies of the Christian right.

21. National Conference of Catholic Bishops, *Pastoral Letter on Catholic Social Teaching and the U.S. Economy*, second draft (Washington, DC: U.S. Catholic Conference, 1985), paragraph 28.

22. Interview with Sally White, legislative director, Concerned Women for America, June 1989.

23. Interview with Matthew Smyth, legislative director, Christian Voice, June 1989.

24. Not for attribution, not included in list of interviews.

25. Matthew C. Moen, *The Transformation of the Christian Right* (Tuscaloosa: University of Alabama Press, 1993), pp. 119–37.

26. Interview with John Carr, secretary of social development and world peace, U.S. Catholic Conference, November 1988.

27. Not for attribution.

28. Interview with Ed Snyder, executive secretary, Friends Committee on National Legislation, November 1988.

29. Interview with Glen Stein, associate director, Union of American Hebrew Congregations, November 1988.

30. Interview with John Carr, secretary of social development and world peace, U.S. Catholic Conference, November 1988.

31. Quoted in Michael Ferber, "Religious Revival on the Left," *The Nation* 241 (July 6/13, 1985): 12.

32. Quoted in Hertzke, *Representing God in Washington,* pp. 234–35.

CHAPTER 7

1. For a discussion of the popular support of one branch of fundamentalism, the Moral Majority, see Emmett H. Buell and Lee Sigelman, "An Army That Meets Every Sunday? Popular Support for the Moral Majority," *Social Science Quarterly* 66 (June 1985): 427–34; Anson Schupe and Wil-

liam Stacey, "The Moral Majority Constituency," in *The New Christian Right*, ed. Robert Liebman and Robert Wuthnow (New York: Aldine, 1983); and Allen Hertzke, "The Role of Religious Lobbies," in *Religion in American Politics*, ed. Charles W. Dunn (Washington, DC: CQ Press, 1989), pp. 130–34.

2. Despite this rash of statements, it is important to note that U.S. policy did not change until public opinion began to change in 1968.

3. James Luther Adams, *The Growing Church Lobby in Washington* (Grand Rapids, MI: Eerdmans, 1970), p. 244.

4. James Reichley, *Religion in American Public Life* (Washington, DC: Brookings Institution, 1985), pp. 269–74.

5. Anne Motley Hallum, "Presbyterians as Political Amateurs," in Charles W. Dunn, ed., *Religion in American Politics* (Washington, DC: CQ Press, 1989), pp. 64–66.

6. Mary Hanna, *Catholics and American Politics* (Cambridge, MA: Harvard University Press, 1979).

7. Frank J. Sorauf, *The Wall of Separation* (Princeton, NJ: Princeton University Press, 1976), p. 185.

8. Jeffrey Hadden, *The Gathering Storm in the Churches* (Garden City, NY: Doubleday, 1969); and Harold E. Quinley, *The Prophetic Clergy: Social Activism among Protestant Ministers* (New York: John Wiley, 1974).

9. Ari L. Goldman, "Church Council, Losing Appeal, Adopts Changes; Liberal Protestants Seek to Reach Out to Rivals," *New York Times*, November 4, 1988.

10. American National Election Study, Survey Research Center-Center for Political Studies, University of Michigan, Ann Arbor, 1984.

11. Allen Hertzke, *Representing God in Washington: The Role of Religious Lobbies* (Knoxville: University of Tennessee Press, 1988), pp. 117–60.

12. Political scientists call opportunities to meet new people a "solidary benefit." Providing for personal spiritual growth or political lobbying with member support is termed a "purposive benefit."

13. American National Election Study, Survey Research Center-Center for Political Studies, University of Michigan, Ann Arbor, 1988.

14. See Lawrence S. Rothenberg, "Agenda Setting at Common Cause," in Allan J. Cigler and Burdett A. Loomis, eds., *Interest Group Politics*, 3rd ed. (Washington, DC: CQ Press, 1991), for a fuller development of the concept, relevant public.

15. Since mainline Protestants work in coalition together on most issues, this consensus is not surprising. Most of them have offices together in the Methodist building across the street from the Capitol. The coalitions in which they work together include the Washington Interreligious Staff Council (WISC), IMPACT, the National Council of Churches, and the Interfaith Coalition for Economic Justice.

16. Although abortion has been a low-priority issue for mainline Protestant lobbyists, mainline Protestants have been occasionally active on the school prayer issue. In 1984 there was some testimony and other action, but it has never been a priority issue.

17. It may have been earlier in the 1980s during the beginning of the Reagan administration defense buildup.

18. Samuel S. Hill and Dennis E. Owen, *The New Religious Right in America* (Nashville, TN: Abingdon, 1982); Matthew C. Moen, *The Christian Right and Congress* (Tuscaloosa: University of Alabama Press, 1989).

19. The data on fundamentalist opinion are not drawn from direct surveys of members. Thus the measure is not completely valid. But since the fundamentalist members of churches in the American National Election Survey data are the major targets for the recruitment of members, the data provide a reasonable surrogate for a direct member survey.

20. See Timothy A. Byrnes, *Catholic Bishops in American Politics* (Princeton, NJ: Princeton University Press, 1991), for a more complete discussion of the relationship between Catholic bishops and elected officials on the issue of abortion.

21. There is one Catholic organization, Catholics for a Free Choice, that is explicitly prochoice.

22. Thomas J. O'Hara has written about other Catholic groups in Washington. These groups provide additional diversity for Catholics. However, the groups that O'Hara adds are, for the most part, small groups that do not engage in significant amounts of lobbying. See his article, "The Multifaceted Catholic Lobby," in *Religion in American Politics,* ed. Dunn.

23. George Gallup, Jr., and Jim Castelli, *The People's Religion* (New York: Macmillan, 1989), p. 170.

24. Interview with John Carr, U.S. Catholic Conference, November 1988.

25. National Conference of Catholic Bishops, *Economic Justice for All: Pastoral Letter on Catholic Social Teaching and the U.S. Economy* (Washington, DC: National Conference of Catholic Bishops, 1986)

26. National Conference of Catholic Bishops, "The Challenge of Peace: God's Promise and Our Response," *Origins,* May 19, 1983, p. 2.

27. For a more detailed analysis of the process of drafting the pastoral letter on the economy, see Mary Hanna, "The Dance of Legislation: Church Style," in Ted G. Jelen, ed., *Religion and Political Behavior in the United States* (New York: Praeger, 1989).

28. The sensitivity of Catholic bishops to member opinion is shown by a comparison of the letters on public policy produced by the Canadian and U.S. bishops. True to their political tradition, the U.S. bishops did not recommend any socialist options. The Canadian bishops did.

29. *The Gallup Report,* Nos. 244–245, 254, 1986.

30. Interview with Mark Pelavin, associate Washington representative, American Jewish Congress, November 1988.

31. Interview with Glen Stein, associate director, Union of American Hebrew Congregations, November 1988.

32. Interview with Donna MortonStout, associate general secretary, Washington Office of the United Methodist Church, November 1988.

33. Interview with Mary Jane Patterson, director, General Board of Church and Society, Presbyterian Church–U.S.A., November 1988.

34. Ibid.

35. Interview with Robert Brooks, presiding bishop's staff officer, Washington Office of the Episcopal Church, November 1988.

36. Interview with Richard Cizik, issue director, National Association of Evangelicals, November 1988.

37. Interview with Arthur Simon, executive director, Bread for the World, and Nancy Sylvester, national coordinator, NETWORK, November 1988.

38. Interview with Sally Timmel, coordinator, Church Women United, June 1988.

39. See Robert Godwin, *The Direct Marketing of Politics: 500 Million Dollars of Influence* (Chatham, NJ: Chatham House, 1987), for evidence that showed the Moral Majority shifting their position on the basis of member response.

40. Kay Lehman Schlozman and John Tierney, *Organized Interests and American Democracy* (New York: Harper & Row, 1986), p. 139. Schlozman and Tierney note that V. O. Key offers a fuller expression of that view. Other theorists including E. E. Schattschneider also develop this argument.

41. See Ellen M. Rosenberg, *The Southern Baptists: A Subculture in Transition* (Knoxville: University of Tennessee Press, 1989), for a fuller discussion of the internal conflicts within the Southern Baptist Convention.

42. Interview with Matthew Ahman, associate director for governmental relations, Catholic Charities, November 1988.

43. Interview with Mark Pelavin, associate Washington representative, American Jewish Congress, November 1988.

44. Interview with Arthur Simon, executive director, Bread for the World, November 1988.

45. Interview with Leland Wilson, director, Washington Office of the Church of the Brethren, November 1988.

CHAPTER 8

1. Cf. Sydney E. Mead, *The Nation with the Soul of a Church* (New York: Harper & Row, 1975).

2. Garry Wills, *Under God: Religion and Politics in America* (New York: Simon and Schuster, 1990).

3. Fred Barnes, "The New Covenant," *The New Republic*, November 9, 1992, pp. 32–33.

4. Paul Tillich, *Dynamics of Faith* (New York: Harper & Row, 1957).

5. Martin Marty made this point in a public lecture at Grace Lutheran Church, Apple Valley, Minnesota, October 31, 1993. See also Martin E. Marty and R. Scott Appleby, eds., *Fundamentalisms and Society: Reclaiming the Sciences, the Family, and Education*, vol. 2, and *Fundamentalisms and the State: Remaking Polities, Economies, and Militance*, vol. 3 (Chicago: University of Chicago Press, 1993).

6. In Frank S. Mead, *Handbook of Denominations*, 7th ed. (Nashville, TN: Abingdon, 1971), there is a list of the addresses of more than 200 denominational headquarters in the United States. Many additional religious organizations do not have a denominational headquarters.

7. See Kay Lehman Schlozman and John Tierney, *Organized Interests and American Democracy* (New York: Harper &

Row, 1986), pp. 148–62; and Ronald J. Hrebenar and Ruth K. Scott, *Interest Group Politics in America*, 2nd ed. (Englewood Cliffs, NJ: Prentice Hall, 1990), chs. 4 and 5.

8. See Allen D. Hertzke, "Christian Fundamentalists and the Imperatives of American Politics," in Emile Sahliyeh, *Religious Resurgence and Politics in the Contemporary World*, (Albany, NY: State University of New York Press, 1990) for a discussion of the moderation of American fundamentalists.

9. See Steve Bruce, *The Rise and Fall of the New Christian Right: Conservative and Protestant Politics in America, 1978–1988* (New York: Oxford University Press, 1988) and Matthew C. Moen, *The Christian Right and Congress* (Tuscaloosa: University of Alabama Press, 1989).

10. Kevin Phillips, *The Politics of Rich and Poor: Wealth and the American Electorate in the Reagan Aftermath* (New York: Random House, 1990).

APPENDIX

1. The current interpretation of legal statutes says that organizations may not devote more than 20 percent of their total resources to lobbying. Because most religious lobbying organizations are part of much larger churches and denominations, they can devote all the resources of their Washington offices and still maintain their 501(c)3 status.

2. See Garry Wills, *Under God: Religion and Politics in America* (New York: Simon and Schuster, 1990), pp. 15–25, for a fuller criticism of the treatment of religion by journalists. Wills is a professor of American culture at Northwestern University and a journalist who has written for many pub-

lications including *Time, The New York Review of Books, GQ,* and *American Heritage.*

3. Steven J. Taylor and Robert Bogdan, *Introduction to Qualitative Research Methods: The Search for Meanings* (New York: John Wiley and Sons, 1984), p. 2.

4. Allen Hertzke, *Representing God in Washington: The Role of Religious Lobbies* (Knoxville: University of Tennessee Press, 1988), and Robert Zwier, "The World and Worldview of Religious Lobbyists," paper presented at the 1988 meeting of the Midwest Political Science Association, Chicago, April 4–6.

5. Arthur C. Close and Jody Curtis, eds., *Washington Representatives, 1990* (Washington, DC: Columbia Books, 1985).

6. Paul J. Weber and W. Landis Jones, *U.S. Religious Interest Groups: Institutional Profiles* (Westport, CT: Greenwood Press, 1994).

INDEX